ARE YOUR LIGHTS ON?

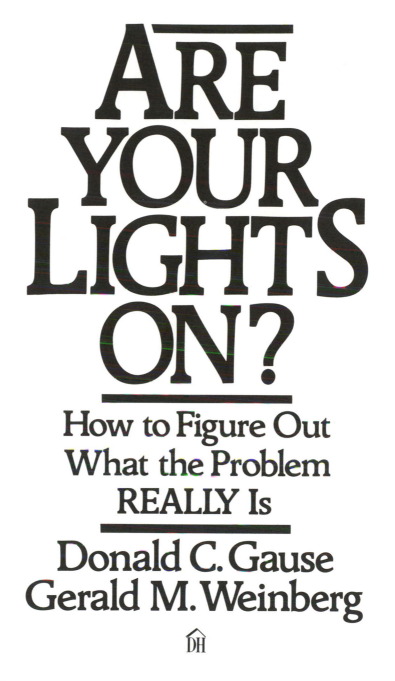

ARE YOUR LIGHTS ON?

How to Figure Out What the Problem REALLY Is

Donald C. Gause
Gerald M. Weinberg

DH

Dorset House Publishing, 353 West 12th Street, New York, NY 10014

For information about Newbridge's audio products, write to:
Newbridge Book Clubs, 3000 Cindel Drive, Delran, NJ 08370

Cover design: Jeff Faville, Faville Graphics,
New York, N.Y.
Interior illustrations: Sally Cox, Lincoln, Neb.
Reprint: Originally published: Cambridge, Mass.:
Winthrop Publishers, © 1982.

Printed in the United States of America

Library of Congress Catalog Number 89-81915
ISBN: 0-932633-16-1

This book is dedicated to our loving wives,
one of whom had to put up with us
while the other had to put up without us
during this relaxation.
It isn't clear which of them
benefited more by the arrangement.

CONTENTS

PREFACE

PROBLEM: Nobody reads prefaces.

SOLUTION: Call the preface Chapter 1.

NEW PROBLEM CREATED BY SOLUTION: Chapter 1 is boring.

RESOLUTION: Throw away Chapter 1 and call Chapter 2 Chapter 1.

PART 1 :

What is the problem?

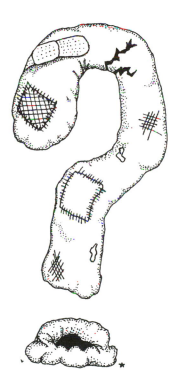

1

A PROBLEM

In the heart of Gotham City's financial district stands the glistening new 73-story Brontosaurus Tower. Even though this architectural masterpiece is not yet fully occupied, the elevator service has been found woefully inadequate by the tenants. Some tenants have actually threatened to leave if the service isn't improved, and quickly.

A few facts of the case are as follows:

(1)   The building primarily houses offices doing business during the weekday hours of 9am to 5pm.

(2)   Nearly everyone using the building is associated in some way with the financial world.

(3)   The occupants are fairly uniformly distributed over the 73 floors, and so is the elevator traffic.

(4)   The owner has invested heavily in advertising in an attempt to rent the remaining office space.

(5)   Discouraging words spread like lightning in the tight little world of the financial district.

WHAT IS TO BE DONE ABOUT THIS SITUATION?

A PROBLEM

A number of ideas spring immediately to mind, such as:

(1)   Speed up the elevators.

(2)   Add elevators by cutting new shafts through the building.

(3)   Add elevators by constructing outside shafts.

(4)   Stagger working hours to spread the rush hour load over a longer period.

(5)   Move occupants to different floors to reduce total passenger traffic within the building.

(6)   Restrict the number of people entering the building.

(7)   Replace existing elevators with bigger cars stretching two or three stories.

(8)   Provide more services locally on each floor to reduce floor-to-floor traffic.

(9)   Reschedule the elevators with special local and express arrangements, as needed.

Having followed our natural problem-solving tendencies, we have rushed right into solutions. Perhaps it would be wiser to ask a few questions before stating answers.

What sorts of questions? *Who* has the problem? What *is* the problem? Or, at this juncture, just what is *a problem?*
Consider the question, "Whose problem is it?" This question attempts to

(1)   determine who is the client—that is, who must be made happy.

(2)   establish some clues that may lead to appropriate solutions.

Our first list of solutions, diverse as they were, all shared a single point of view—that the elevator *users* were the people with the problem.
Suppose we try taking the point of view of Mr. Diogenes Diplodocus, the landlord. With him as our client, we might develop a rather different list, such as:

(1)   Increase the rents, so fewer occupants will be needed to pay off the mortgage.

(2)   Convince the occupants that Brontosaurus Tower is a terrific leisurely place to work *because* of the elevator situation.

(3)   Convince the occupants that they need more exercise—which they could get by walking the stairs rather than riding the elevators—by posting walking times and calorie consumption estimates over well-traveled routes.

(4)   Burn down the building and collect the fire insurance.

(5)   Sue the builder.

(6)   Steal elevator time from the next-door neighbor.

These two lists, though not necessarily mutually exclusive, do show somewhat different orientations. This difference should arrest our natural tendency to produce hasty solutions before asking

WHAT IS THE PROBLEM?

The fledgling problem solver invariably rushes in with solutions before taking time to define the problem being solved. Even experienced solvers, when subjected to social pressure, yield to this demand for haste. When they do, many solutions are found, but not necessarily to the problem at hand. As each person competes for acceptance of a favored solution, each one accuses the other of stubbornness, not of having an alternative point of view.

Not every problem-solving group founders on lack of attention to definition. Some come to grief by endlessly circling around attempted definitions, **never** amassing the courage to get on with the solution in spite of definitional dangers.

As a practical matter, it is impossible to define natural, day-to-day problems in a single, unique, totally unambiguous fashion. On the other hand, without **some** common understanding of the problem, a solution will almost invariably be to the **wrong** problem. Usually, it will be the problem of the person who talks loudest, or most effectively. Or who has the biggest bank account.

For the would-be problem solver, whose problem is to solve the problems of others, the best way to begin is mentally to **shift gears from singular to plural**—from Problem

7

ARE YOUR LIGHTS ON?

Solver to Problems Solver, or, if you find that hard to pronounce, to Solver of Problems.

   To practice this mental shift, the Solver should, early in the game, try to answer the question:

WHO HAS A PROBLEM?

and then, for each unique answering party, to ask

WHAT IS THE ESSENCE OF YOUR PROBLEM?

2

PETER PIGEONHOLE PREPARES A PETITION

From the perspective of the office workers, the Brontosaurus problem might be stated as

HOW CAN I COVER MY APPOINTED ROUNDS WITH MINIMUM TIME, EFFORT, AND/OR AGGRAVATION?

For Mr. Diplodocus, the problem may be abstracted to

HOW CAN I DISPOSE OF ALL THESE BLANKETY-BLANK COMPLAINTS?

If these two parties (are there others?) cannot get together, a mutually satisfactory solution seems improbable. Unpleasant as the prospect may be, an effective problems solver must work towards achieving a meeting—if not of minds, then of bodies.

In order to call the landlord's attention to "the problem," a mailboy at Finicky Financial Fiduciary, Peter Pigeonhole, prepares a petition. Using his role as mailboy, he is able to obtain an impressive list of signatures at 3F. Using his class connections with other firms' mailboys, he expands the list.

Peter needs many signatures because a petition is exactly what Diplodocus *doesn't* want. *His* problem as he sees it, is to *eliminate* complaints. If complaints are never recorded, but merely mumbled and grumbled into the air, he may be able to solve his problem by ignoring it. Who knows? This may turn out to be a phantom problem! Therefore, even when faced with four-and-twenty signatures baked into a petition, he does nothing. More precisely, he returns the petition envelope marked REFUSED BY ADDRESSEE.

Trying to discourage a mailboy by refusing a letter is like trying to discourage a capitalist bull by waving a Russian flag. The landlord's solution merely infuriates the office workers. In retaliation, they escalate. (Now there's an idea!)

A large group of representatives pays a call on Mr. Diplodocus, who continues to solve *his* problem by pretending ignorance. He is, his secretary says, "not in."

If Diplodocus thought this tactic would discourage the petitioners, he was sadly misinformed about the persistence of mailboys in making their appointed rounds. After some discussion of tactics, the group decides to visit Diplodocus at his Scarsdale Estate. To help deliver their message, they bring four picket signs, three stink bombs, and two immigrant workers. Mrs. Diplodocus speaks sharply to Mr. Diplodocus, and it's a phantom problem no longer.

After a brief meeting with a worker delegation, Diplodocus agrees to hire a consulting firm to look into the problem. In return, the pickets are sent home, which solves his immediate problem with Mrs. Diplodocus.

Time passes. The workers can discern no improvement—and not even a trace of a consultant. Wouldn't you think there would be a few short-haired guys in bowties standing around with clipboards asking questions? At the very least, Diplodocus could have hired his nephew to stand around in a turtleneck with a calculator.

ARE YOUR LIGHTS ON?

Upon investigation, Peter Pigeonhole discovers that the landlord has not yet gotten around to hiring the consulting firm. Unable to afford daily trips to Scarsdale, the workers decide upon a new tactic.

Using their privileged positions as mailboys, the protest leaders circulate a rumor that if the elevator situation isn't solved soon, the American Congress of Labor is going to organize the entire clerical workforce in Brontosaurus Tower. Until now, the management of each tenant firm hasn't been too concerned with the elevator situation. *They* arrive early and stay late, or arrive late and leave early. Their secretaries fetch coffee, a caterer produces lunch, and the mailboys "gopher" the mail and other essentials. Moreover, though Men's and Women's Conveniences are located on alternate floors, each floor has a small, locked, well-appointed Restroom whose use is restricted to Executive Gentlemen. (There are no Executive Ladies in Brontosaurus).

Once the ACL organizing rumor starts, it spreads like a muscle spasm in management's lower back. Suddenly there are *three* parties to the problem, and party three—the management—begins to apply its own brand of persuasion to party two—the landlord.

Up until now, neither party was willing to agree with the other's definition. Or even to listen to it. Now, however, we can discern the signs of progress. When one party begins to feel pain in synchrony with the other, we know that the problem will eventually find its resolution.

The American Indians have a name for this problem-solving technique—it's called "walking in the other person's moccasins." It works especially well when the moccasins are wet rawhide, dried slowly on the other person's feet until sufficient sympathy ("feeling together") is achieved.

PETER PIGEONHOLE PREPARES A PETITION

We can't predict, at this juncture, just *how* the problem will achieve its resolution. The tenant's lawyers may abrogate the leases or escrow the rent. The landlord may sell the building at a loss and/or leap out of the 73rd story. New problems may be created by such resolutions, but one thing is now certain: the previous problems are not long for this world.

Out of the multiplicity of diverse outcomes, let's assume that all concerned parties have sufficiently cool heads to attempt to act rationally. The landlord and the lawyers meet to decide upon the nature of the problem. At the last moment, a workers' representative is grudgingly admitted under threat of ACL intervention. After a bit of righteous posturing, all parties recognize the need for more information.

Mr. Diplodocus has mentally discarded all previous complaints, but is unable to construct any particular pattern other than his original impression that the workers were chronic complainers.

The management hasn't really thought about the problem for long, or in much detail. To them, it is a tangential problem, though now quite real, to their direct abhorrence of any form of organized labor.

The workers, for their part, are so obsessed with their desire to "get that SOB landlord" that they have forgotten their original interest in improving the elevator service.

Without wallowing in the messy details, we can report that the meeting resulted in agreement among all parties that

(1)   The landlord is unhappy because of the harassment.

(2)   The tenant firms are unhappy because of their employees' unhappiness and resultant threats of unionization.

13

(3)   The workers are unhappy because of the way the landlord has ignored their pleas, and because of poor elevator service.

From this perspective, there are now *three* problems, at least.
    Cut in a different direction, the problem still appears threefold:

(1)   How can we determine "What is wrong?"

(2)   What *is* wrong?

(3)   What can be done about it?

The first part of the question is quickly resolved. Peter Pigeonhole is assigned the job of finding out what is wrong. He will define the problem in a manner acceptable to all parties. For this task, 3F agrees to relieve him of mailroom duties for one month. Such is the reward for taking the initiative—now it's *his* problem.

WHAT WOULD YOU DO IF YOU WERE IN THE MOCCASINS OF PETER PIGEONHOLE?

3

WHAT'S YOUR PROBLEM?

Have you ever had a day when things didn't go your way and you found yourself saying, "Boy, have I got problems!"? Most people do, and some do almost every day. The difficulty they feel is a discrepancy between the way things are going and "their way"—the way they *should* be going, in one person's opinion. It's quite natural to describe this situation by saying, "Boy, have I got problems!"—because a problem is neither more nor less than such a discrepancy.

A PROBLEM IS A DIFFERENCE
BETWEEN THINGS AS *DESIRED*
AND THINGS AS *PERCEIVED*

If you raise your nose from this book and look about you, you can probably list dozens or hundreds of "differences between things desired and things perceived." In fact, why not try it?

Suppose you've just finished a magnificent dinner, settled down in your most comfortable chair, and opened this book to precisely this point in the text. Your sense of well-being is so pervasive that you are unable to think of a single "problem," let alone hundreds. Yet chances are that if you turn up your sensitivity ever so slightly, you might recognize the following discrepancies between perception and desire:

ARE YOUR LIGHTS ON?

PERCEPTION	DESIRE
This chair is wearing out.	Brand new chair.
The kids are too noisy.	Quiet children.
Your feet are aching.	Comfortable moccasins.
The house is too cool.	Warmer house.
The house is too warm.	Cooler house.

The first three listed problems will probably be solved by employing the ancient but effective method of "ignoring the problem." This method is neither more nor less than turning down our sensitivity. At some point, we no longer perceive any difference between things as they are and things as we want them to be. Moreover, the problem of the cold house, now that you've recognized it, will most likely be solved by turning up the thermostat or, in these days of "energy crisis," putting on a sweater.

But suppose you look at the thermostat and find the room to be at 25° C (77° F)—quite warm enough for any "normal" person. Do you still have a problem? Definitely YES—so long as the temperature as perceived is not the temperature as desired. Seeing the "objective" temperature doesn't help a thing—unless you can convince yourself that you're really warm enough after all. In that case, we could consider the problem of warmth to be a *phantom problem*—a discomfort primarily attributable to perceptions.

But don't be misled:

PHANTOM PROBLEMS ARE REAL PROBLEMS.

Faced with a room temperature of 25° C and a feeling of being too cold, you may decide you are "coming down with something." You might go straight to bed, or take a pill or a drink, or both, or make an appointment with your family doctor (for next October).

16

WHAT'S YOUR PROBLEM?

In any case, the problem, originally formulated as "the house is too cold," now takes another form, such as, "Why am I imagining that the house is too cold?" or "What is wrong with my body?"

"Yes, yes," you're muttering from your worn chair, "but my children are banging on the walls, my feet are killing me, and something's wrong with the furnace. I haven't got a lot of time to waste, but I can't put this book down until I find out what happened to the Brontosaurus Tower Problem. Get on with it! Get on with it!"

Very well, then, back to Peter Pigeonhole. He's just been reading a book on problem solving—from which he's learned that

A PROBLEM IS A DIFFERENCE
BETWEEN THING AS *DESIRED*
AND THINGS AS *PERCEIVED*

Armed with this profound insight (profound to a mailboy, at least) Peter turned back to the Brontosaurus problem. What was *desired,* he reasoned, was a short wait for the elevators. What was *perceived* was too long a wait.

Seen in this way, the problem could be solved either by changing desires or changing perceptions. He could alter the perceptions by shortening the actual waiting time, or by making the time *seem* shorter. And just when he came to this realization, Peter chanced to read about a similar problem in one of his problem-solving books. In this situation, employees were getting injured running down the stairs after work. The problem was solved by putting a mirror on each landing. In their vanity, the employees slowed their relentless charge for the exits, in order to check their appearance and make minor adjustments.

"Perhaps," Peter reasoned, "a similar device would solve our own problem." Peter's employers were happy to hear that he had come up with something, for the mail wasn't being delivered too well in his absence. Mr. Diplodocus was so pleased that it wouldn't cost very much that he immediately agreed to have mirrors installed alongside the elevators on each floor. Sure enough, complaints fell immediately, and Peter was given a large pat on the back, a small raise, and his old desk in the mailroom.

Alas, alas, the grubby world of Gotham City has little in common with the immaculate world of books on problem solving. Before long, the ubiquitous "vandals" discovered that Brontosaurus Tower had more mirrors than Versailles. Within weeks, Peter was put back on special assignment, trying to figure out what to do about graffiti on the mirrors.

Having been addicted to this pernicious vice by his previous exposure, he was reading another book on problem solving when his new assignment came in. In this treatise, he had learned the concept of trying to find a solution to a problem by "making it worse." "Aha," he saw in a flash, "the problem is not one of grafitti, but of base and unimaginative graffiti. What difference does it make if they slow down to look in the mirror or to look at the graffiti? In either case, they won't notice how slow the elevators are."

Peter now proposed that each floor be supplied with wax crayons (chained to the walls, of course). Everyone could participate in defacing the mirrors, each with his favorite graffito, while waiting for the elevator. Another large pat on the back, another (smaller) raise, and Peter was back in the mailroom savoring his triumph of mind over matter.

As all these events were transpiring, time was passing. Almost before anyone noticed it, Brontosaurus Tower attain-

ed its first birthday. As the law of Gotham City required, the engineers from Uplift Elevator arrived one morning to make their annual inspection.

As soon as they saw the hordes of workers milling about the lobby, crayons in hand, they sensed a difference between the things *they* perceived and the things *they* desired. Their professional pride was at stake, for their company's slogan was

NOBODY

WAITS

FOR

A

LIFT

UP

FROM

UPLIFT

"Something must be amiss with the controls," one told the other, "for Uplift elevators simply can't cause crowds like this if they're working properly."

Thereupon, the engineers set to work locating the problem. Lo and behold, they discovered that a rat had been trapped in the master control box the day the elevator system was installed. In his futile efforts to gnaw his way out, he had clamped down on a master relay with the full force of his tiny jaws. He was rewarded with 240 volts that not only saved him from slow death by starvation, but which also embalmed him and the master relay in a permanently closed position. It was a simple—though disgusting—job to remove the rat and replace the relay, after which the engineers checked out the system and found it now working to Uplift standards.

Before departing until next year's inspection, they paid a call on Mr. Diplodocus. Laying the embalmed rat on his desk, they said, haughtily, "If you can't keep your building clean, you could at least get in touch with us when you see the elevators running so slow.. Don't you realize you could lose your tenants over such poor service?"

"Well," thought the landlord, "at least they've finally solved the problem once and for all." Having just that morning received a petition from the Brontosaurus chapter of the Legion of Decency complaining about the graffiti, he knew that the previous "solution" was about to collapse right under his feet. He breathed a sigh of relief and escorted the engineers to the front door. It was almost five o'clock, and he wanted to see how happy the workers would be when they discovered the improved service.

No sooner had the quitting bell sounded than employees began streaming from their offices to the elevators, each hoping to be the first on his floor to get to the crayons. With the properly working elevators, however, people were swept down to the ground floor before they had a chance to write "fiddlesticks". Without the retarded elevators to spread the rush of hundreds of workers over a fifteen or twenty-minute interval, everyone hit the subway entrance at once—far more rapidly than the Interminable Racket Transit could handle. In the ensuing crush, five people fainted from the heat, seven were hospitalized with heelholes in their feet, and poor Mr. Diplodocus was shoved down the stairs, right through the ticket gate, and out onto the platform.

Because the subway didn't go to Scarsdale, Diplodocus had never before been inside a subway station. Untrained in the proper elbowing technique, he couldn't defend himself and was jostled off the platform directly into the path of the onrushing Express.

The funeral was well attended by management and workers alike, for, in attempting to solve the elevator problem, they had come to know and respect their landlord,

greedy little tyrant though he was. In order to demonstrate that there were no hard feelings concerning their previous differences, Peter Pigeonhole was asked to deliver a eulogy to Mr. Diplodocus on behalf of the occupants of Brontosaurus Tower.

Peter began his discourse by relating the events of the past year, and how he had come to know Mr. Diplodocus and appreciate his point of view. In conclusion, Peter said, sadly, "What a pity that he had to come to such a sudden end, just when the elevator problem was finally solved. We never know what problems are—until we don't have them any more."

ARE YOUR LIGHTS ON?

POSTSCRIPT:

As he walked sadly away from the fresh Diplodocus grave, Peter was taken by the arm by a friendly old man who he vaguely recognized. "I'm E. J. Corvair, owner of the department store across the alley from Brontosaurus Tower. That was a moving eulogy you gave old Diplodocus."

"Thank you," said Peter sincerely, glad to find that his message had come across. "I really feel that I let Mr. Diplodocus down, after he put so much faith in my problem-solving ability."

"Oh, you mustn't accuse yourself, young man. When you get to my age, you learn that we have little influence on the *important* matters in our lives."

"Perhaps," Peter replied, "but I do regret some of the things I said to him, particularly when he didn't think I was *serious* enough."

"Such as?"

"I especially remember when I was suggesting far-out solutions, like burning down the building. He really got angry with me then."

"He shouldn't have. Lots of owners burn down their buildings for insurance. The way my business is going right now, I ought to think of that myself."

"Oh, it wasn't *that* suggestion that touched him off. I think he seriously considered that one. What really got him angry was when I suggested stealing elevator time from the building next door."

"But that's really funny," laughed Mr. Corvair. "How could he get angry with such a good joke?"

"Well, he didn't think it was the time or place to be funny, so he threw me out of his office. 'How can you *steal* elevator time from another building?' he asked me, and I couldn't give him a sensible answer, so he threw me out."

WHAT'S YOUR PROBLEM?

"Well, what did you have in mind when you said it?"

"I don't know. It just popped into my head, and it sounded kind of interesting, and funny, so I said it."

"That's too bad," mused Mr. Corvair. "If you *could* take elevator time from one building and use it in another, I'd sure have lots to give you."

"What do you mean?" Peter asked.

"Oh, my business has been so slow that hardly anybody is in the store to use the elevators. We have lots of elevator capacity right next door to Brontosaurus Tower just going to waste."

"But Mr. Corvair!" Peter interrupted, gushing with excitement. "We could build one or two passageways between the two buildings so that people could go into your store to take the elevator if things got crowded! In fact, we could have done that a long time ago."

"If only Diplodocus were alive," Mr. Corvair speculated. "I would offer to build those passageways completely at my expense, just to get the extra business into my store. I'd be more than happy to have you people steal *my* elevator time."

"Well," said Peter optimistically," all is not lost. Perhaps the Diplodocus heirs will be more receptive to the idea than he was!" And so they were, thus teaching Peter yet another valuable lesson:

DON'T BOTHER TRYING TO SOLVE PROBLEMS
FOR PEOPLE WHO DON'T HAVE A SENSE OF HUMOR.

PART 2 :

What is the problem?

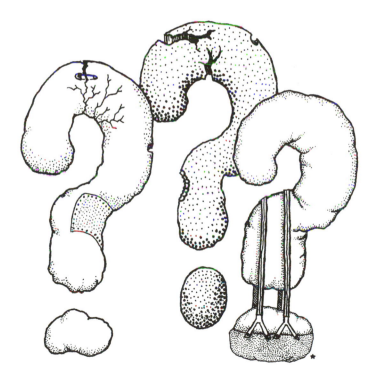

4

BILLY BRIGHTEYES BESTS THE BIDDERS

The computer field is a mother lode of problem definition lessons. In our next story, the client was a large corporation, as represented by its President, Vice-President, and Comptroller. This high level problem-setting group was entirely matched to the magnitude of the problem—one involving purchases of tens of millions of dollars worth of government surplus property.

The purchasing was to be done by a system of sealed bids. Four companies were bidding on a total of eleven properties. Not all properties were equally desirable. Indeed, some of them were not wanted by any of the four companies, but the government had sagely set up a complex series of rules to ensure that all properties were actually sold.

For example, each company, if it wanted to bid at all, had to bid on all eleven properties. If certain bids were not sufficiently high in relation to others, they would automatically be raised to a minimum. Other rules tended to tie the least desirable properties to the most desirable. Consequently, it was not simply the best bid on each property that won, but some combination of good bids on a group of properties.

Because so much money was involved, and so much uncertainty, the executives had become tormented with anxiety or, even worse, curiosity. In this weakened state, they were susceptible to an offer by an enterprising government official—to make the entire set of sealed bids available to them, along with an opportunity to change their bids—for a substantial price.

WHO GETS WHAT?

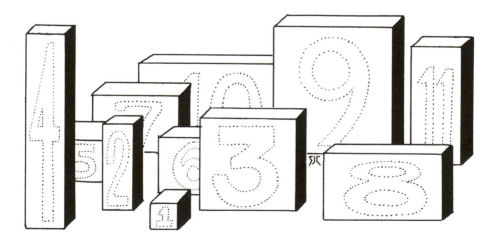

BILLY BRIGHTEYES BESTS THE BIDDERS

They paid the price and opened the bids. To their dismay, the rules were so complex they still couldn't determine who would get which property. By the time they reluctantly decided to seek outside help, they had frittered away all but 24 hours of their allotted time. When the Comptroller arrived at the office of the computing service, he was a tired and desperate man. But he was a man with a plan.

After being assured by the management of the utmost discretion, the Comptroller was introduced to a group of computer programmers, headed by Billy Brighteyes. Billy listened carefully as he presented his blueprint for a computer program to relieve his anxieties. Since there were 11 properties and 4 sets of bids, he figured out that there were 4^{11}—or approximately 4,000,000—different combinations of bids. (The ability to make this kind of approximation is essential to problem solvers. We shall take it up in another book. For now, if you don't understand where the numbers come from, just take it on faith. Or you can check with some mathematical friend.)

Each of the 4,000,000 combinations would result in some total revenue to the government, which would presumably choose that combination fitting all the rules and yielding the most money to the public treasury. The Comptroller's plan was to have the computer generate all 4,000,000 bid combinations, then arrange them in order with the highest revenues coming first. The executive committee would then peruse this list from top to bottom, in order to find the highest combination that met all the rules.

BID POSSIBILITIES REPORT

	PROPERTY NUMBER											GOV'T REVENUE
	1	2	3	4	5	6	7	8	9	10	11	
WHICH												
COMPANY	B	C	A	A	D	B	D	A	A	C	B	$187,926,351
GETS	C	B	A	A	D	C	D	B	A	C	B	$184,897,680
THIS	C	B	B	A	D	C	C	B	A	B	D	$183,102,395
PROPERTY	D	B	B	A	D	B	C	B	B	B	D	$180,090,444
	B	C	A	A	D	B	D	A	A	C	B	$179,580,604
	B	C	A	B	D	C	D	A	A	B	C	$177,203,945
	D	B	A	B	C	C	D	A	B	B	C	$174,381,509
	C	C	B	D	B	A	B	D	A	D	B	$171,284,137

etcetera,
etcetera...
over
4,000,000
etceteras

BILLY BRIGHTEYES BESTS THE BIDDERS

With but 24 hours remaining, and with the computer work alone estimated at 12 hours, there was little time to waste debating the plausibility of this plan. Once the bids were opened, all would be lost. Nevertheless, Billy felt that the method was unnecessarily crude—it offended his problem-solver sense of elegance. He reasoned that a little information about the government's rules could possibly reduce the total computation by a factor of 10. If the computation could actually be done in 1 hour instead of 12, the executives would have much more time to look at a much smaller list.

The Comptroller was hesitant to release any more than the minimum of information. He finally relented when presented with the argument that a faster method might also permit them to predict the outcome of a changed bid. It was agreed that one group of programmers would begin working on the Comptroller's method while Billy Brighteyes went with the Comptroller to look over the bidding regulations—which were in no circumstances to be let out of the company's hands.

After Billy left, the other programmers had a few moments of conscience-searching. Although the Comptroller had never admitted it in so many words, the information on the sealed bids had unmistakably come from some sort of illegal transaction—and although they had never heard anyone say explicitly that it was illegal—could they remain morally neutral if they participated in such shady dealings?

The group was troubled enough to present the question to their manager. He was quick to point out a moral factor they had overlooked—that this company was their third-best customer, and could hardly be refused this service. In the end, however, they more or less allowed the question of morality to evaporate in their fascination with the technical problems presented by producing the list of 4,000,000 items in the minimum time with the quickest and most reliable programming. Thus, like most professional problem solvers, they skirted the moral issue. But, after all, they had never been trained to deal with such issues, so they concentrated on the technical aspects, which was their profession—wasn't it?

About twenty minutes after they had set aside their consciences, Billy returned from the executive suite. They were eager to show him some clever shortcuts they had worked out—steps which would reduce the job cost to about $900. But Billy shushed them with a wave of his hand. He proceeded to relate how he had scanned the bidding rules for a few minutes and then seen how, by the application of a smidgin of formal logic and a smattering of common sense, he had completely solved the problem in less than 5 minutes.

To be sure, it had then taken him 20 more minutes to convince the executives that he indeed had a solution—to the problem they had been working on for days. But it had been worth the time, for Billy had learned two important lessons in problem definition.

DON'T TAKE THEIR SOLUTION METHOD
FOR A PROBLEM DEFINITION

And second,

IF YOU SOLVE THEIR PROBLEM TOO READILY,
THEY'LL NEVER BELIEVE YOU'VE SOLVED
THEIR REAL PROBLEM.

5

BILLY BITES HIS TONGUE

Needless to say, Billy's group of programmers was sorely disappointed that the bidding project was dropped as suddenly as it had begun. Though Billy didn't suspect at the time, the story had not yet run its course. The following year he was transferred to another computing center—one using a different and more powerful computer. As he was being indoctrinated to the new office, he was sent to talk with an operations researcher about "package programs"—prewritten programs which solved standard problems arising in a variety of contexts.

"Of course," the operations researcher told him, "the principal advantage of these packaged solutions is the cost savings, but sometimes there are other advantages."

"You mean like special features and more rigid checking of data?" Billy asked.

"Yes, those too, but I was thinking of a more interesting situation, one where the speed with which we could get a solution was the critical factor. Last year, we got a problem from one of our best customers in connection with some bids for government surplus property. It seems they had managed to obtain the sealed bids of the other companies—we never asked them how, you'll understand—and wanted to find out how well they were going to do. That way, they could change their bid if necessary to get the properties they wanted and not get any inferior properties."

A tiny light went on in Billy's brain. In as innocent a voice as he could muster, he asked, "How many other companies were there?"

"Three others. But there were eleven different properties, which made an enormous number of possible combinations."

"About 4,000,000."

"Say, you're quick. Yes, about 4,000,000. And since time was so short, there was no chance of enumerating all of them. Besides, there were all sorts of crazy conditions on the bidding, which would have made programming much too complex to do in a short time."

"So what did you do?" Billy was truly curious.

"That's just the point—we used a package. In just two days, our linear programming specialist managed to cast the problem into the correct form for our package. After that, a few hours of computer time and we had the answer they wanted. Boy, were they ever pleased—there were millions of dollars at stake."

"That's really interesting. How much did the whole job cost?"

"That's another good part of it. There was two days' time for our linear programming man, which came to $400—plus about $1,000 worth of computer time."

"So, for only $1,400 they had their solution."

"And in less than three days! That's what I mean about the value of package programs. You might say that they're solutions just lying in wait for problems!"

"Yes," said Billy pensively, "you might very well say that."

BILLY BITES HIS TONGUE

What he was thinking, of course, was about an expanded version of a problem definition lesson he had once learned:

DON'T MISTAKE A SOLUTION METHOD FOR A PROBLEM DEFINITION—ESPECIALLY IF IT'S YOUR OWN SOLUTION METHOD.

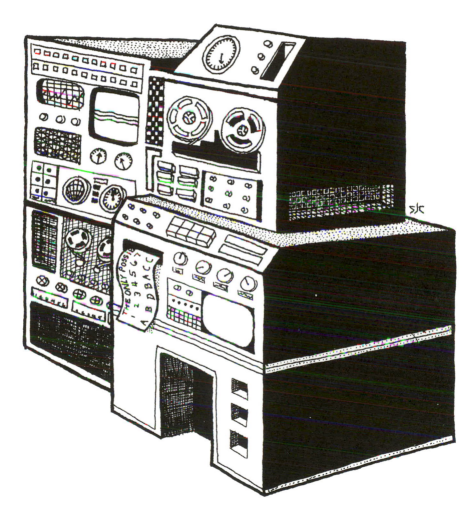

6

BILLY BACK TO THE BIDDERS

As Billy left the office of the operations researcher, his mind wasn't occupied with the subject of package programs, as his host imagined. Instead, it was swirling with far more intriguing questions:

"What about those other two companies?"

"Who had 'solved' their problem—and for how much?"

"And what happened when the ultimate bids, all changed, had been opened? Were they *all* surprised?"

"What did they say or do to the person or persons who sold them the 'secret' bids?"

Billy's mind couldn't rest. He had put the problem away, almost a year ago, thinking he knew all there was to know about it. Now, he realized, the one thing he knew was that the problem was something other than what he then thought. It wasn't a problem of enumerating 4,000,000 cases. Nor was it a problem of symbolic logic and common sense—and especially not one of linear programming.

Perhaps the problem was this: How do you change your bid in a situation when all the others are changing their bids and thinking that they are the only ones who have bought the privilege of doing so? But that couldn't be right, because if one party could figure that out, all the others could, too.

Then, perhaps the problem was deeper: How do you change your bid when all the others are changing their bids with the knowledge that you are changing your bid while knowing that they are changing theirs? But isn't that just the equivalent of secret bidding in the first place?

But wait! If one company *knew* that the others would see its bid—a bid which it could later change—it would try to give a first bid that would *mislead* the others. Did one of the four companies plan to throw the others off by having them buy the "secret" bids? Or perhaps all of them did? In that case, the problem was one of how to create a first bid that would mislead the others in the direction you wanted them to go—without them realizing it.

Billy's mind was spinning like dirty water swirling down the bathtub drain. Just as the "tub" was about to empty, he grasped another fleeting thought: If the problem was a setup, with the first bids merely intended to mislead the other bidders, then the best strategy would be to ignore them and treat the problem as a secret bidding after all! That was too much for Billy's drained brain. He sat down in the first available chair, so dizzy he almost missed the seat. In other words, he thought, the *real* lesson about problem solving is this:

YOU CAN NEVER BE SURE YOU HAVE A CORRECT DEFINITION, EVEN AFTER THE PROBLEM IS SOLVED.

With that thought, Billy was able to pull himself together. As he was walking home to his new apartment, however, he thought again about this "lesson." Suppose, he thought, that *my* problem was to find *the* lesson from all this.

YOU CAN NEVER BE SURE YOU HAVE A CORRECT DEFINITION, EVEN AFTER THE PROBLEM IS SOLVED

BILLY BACK TO THE BIDDERS

Then if this is the real lesson, I can't be sure that *I've* solved the right problem—in which case, I can't be sure it *is* the real lesson. Billy sat down on a retaining wall and assumed the posture of Rodin's Thinker. Suppertime came and went. The sunset was spectacular, but Billy saw none of it. Streetlights went on, traffic grew, faded, grew and faded again.

Finally, a streetsweeper left his barrel and broom and spoke softly to Billy. "Hey, buddy, are you all right?"

Billy should have been startled, but wasn't. Instead, the streetsweeper's words gave him just the clue he needed to unravel his tightly knotted skein of thought. "Uh...No. No, I'm not *all* right—but that's all right! Thanks a lot."

With that, Billy stood up, shook the hand of the puzzled sweeper, and set off gingerly for home. "Thinking's not easy," he thought. "Why, I'd bet that if I traced down the outcome of that bidding, I'd find that the government eventually made a mistake in the computation—so all their calculations and plotting didn't make any difference at all. And just because they'd all cheated, they were in no position to question the government's calculations! But, if one of them had taken a *moral* position in the first place, they'd have had clean hands and could have brought the whole episode to a profitable conclusion. So there's a lesson that's *always* worth remembering:"

DON'T LEAP TO CONCLUSIONS, BUT DON'T IGNORE YOUR FIRST IMPRESSION.

But it was an even deeper lesson that made Billy realize he was all right, even though he had been fooled several times concerning the "true" problem definition. The important *question,* he had known for some time, was simply

WHAT IS THE PROBLEM?

ARE YOUR LIGHTS ON?

Where Billy and others had gone wrong was in thinking that if the *question* was important, then the *answer* had to be important, too. "Nope," Billy said to himself as he absent-mindedly emptied his mailbox, "that's not it at all. The *really* important thing in dealing with problems is to know that the question is *never* answered, but that it doesn't matter, as long as you keep asking. It's only when you fool yourself into thinking you have the final problem definition— the final, true answer—that you can be fooled into thinking you have the final solution. And if you think that, you're always wrong, because there is no such thing as a 'final solution.'"

With that, Billy's mind was at rest—not stopped, but at rest. After a good night's sleep, he went downtown and had a bronze plaque made up for his desk, inscribed with these words:

YOU CAN NEVER BE SURE
YOU HAVE A CORRECT DEFINITION,
BUT DON'T EVER STOP TRYING TO GET ONE.

POSTSCRIPT: *The story of Billy and the bids is a true one, disguised so that nobody on the outside would recognize the events of twenty years ago. But somewhere in this happy land there probably are at least two other problem solvers who will recognize the story. Publishing this story after all these years is just another part of our unending quest for an even more correct definition. Will we hear from those others? You never know!*

PART 3 :

What is the problem really?

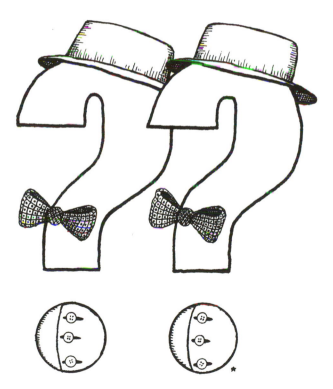

7

THE ENDLESS CHAIN

At one of our large computer manufacturers, a new printer was being developed that was both faster and more accurate than any of its predecessors. The higher speed was easily obtained with the new technology, but the engineering group was having trouble maintaining the accuracy of the printing. Lines sometimes turned out wavy or, when straight, didn't align properly on preprinted forms. Every time a new test was run, the engineers had to spend considerable time in the unrewarding task of measuring the printed output for accuracy.

Dan Daring, the youngest but probably brightest engineer in the group, suggested that they might design a tool that would imprint, impregnate, or otherwise mark an 8-inch interval on computer printout paper. The marks made by the tool were to be the standard reference marks, and would measure any alignment errors quickly and accurately.

Several of the group members worked on ideas for this tool, but most of them got stuck in their thinking because they were preoccupied with the idea of *printing* as the only method of marking on paper. Since they were experienced printer designers, this concept was only natural. Dan Daring, being less experienced with printing, came up with a startling and effective new approach. His final solution was the aluminum bar shown below. Small pins were embedded to punch tiny holes at precisely the prescribed points.

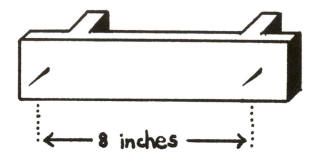

←——— 8 inches ———→

The tool proved easy to build, and was both sturdy and accurate. Time previously wasted on marking the standard intervals was turned to more productive work. Dan's manager was elated. After several weeks had demonstrated the labor savings of this device, the manager decided to recommend Dan for a special company award. He got one of the tools from the shop and brought it to his office so he could study it while writing up his report.

Unfortunately, when he set the tool on his desk, he placed it not on its side, as shown above, but on its "legs," as shown below.

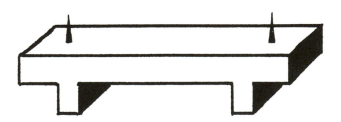

THE ENDLESS CHAIN

Perhaps if Dan's boss had been to India to see the fakirs sitting on beds of nails, he wouldn't have set the tool down that way, but he did. Perhaps if Dan's boss's boss had *been* a fakir, he wouldn't have felt anything when he sat down on the corner of the desk for a friendly chat about Dan's impending award. Alas, neither of these suppositions proved correct, and the entire department was alarmed to hear the Section Chief's agonized scream as two holes, precisely eight inches apart, were punched in his posterior.

The Section Chief, fortunately, had lots of padding in the part of his anatomy that was so accurately marked. Even so, Dan's chances of an award were punctured just as accurately as the Section Chief was punctured. Indeed, the Chief wanted to throw out the whole tool, and perhaps Dan with it, until Dan's manager saved the day by suggesting a simple modification to the tool. By grinding the "legs" into semi-circles, he made it impossible to stand the tool on them with the needles pointing dangerously upward. The only practical way to "stand" the tool was on its side, as shown below.

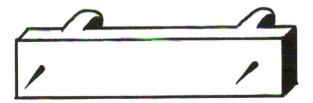

THE ENDLESS CHAIN

Since any problem is a difference between a perceived state and a desired state, when we change a state to "solve" a problem, we usually create one or more other problems. Put simply,

EACH SOLUTION IS THE SOURCE OF THE NEXT PROBLEM.

We never get *rid* of problems. Problems, solutions, and new problems weave an endless chain. The best we can hope for is that the problems we substitute are less troublesome than the ones we "solve."

Sometimes, we make the problems less troublesome by putting them in someone else's back yard—or back end. This technique is called PROBLEM DISPLACEMENT, and is often very useful when consciously and conscientiously done. But new problems—more often than not—are created *unconsciously*.

This lack of consciousness is pervasive. We frequently observe that

THE TRICKIEST PART OF CERTAIN PROBLEMS IS JUST RECOGNIZING THEIR EXISTENCE.

Once the danger of the tool was perceived, any number of solutions tumble into our minds. Indeed, the engineers using the tool every day recognized that Dan's tool could be dangerous if left standing on its legs. They adopted the *habit* of laying it on its side, but they failed to think that *other* people might sometimes handle the tool.

Unlike the engineers, those other people would **not** be familiar with the tool's dangers, and thus could quite easily sit on it or puncture a hand. The engineers recognized their **own** safety problem, but failed to see that it could be a problem for someone else—another case of *problem displacement.*

We can't even be **sure** that some new problem wasn't created by the rounded leg design. You might want to think what it could be.

Or should we say, "what **they** can be?" Twin or triplet births may be rare among humans, but among the problems of the world, anything less than a triplet birth is the rarity. Indeed, one of the most important rules for the would-be problem solver is this:

**IF YOU CAN'T THINK OF AT LEAST THREE THINGS
THAT MIGHT BE WRONG
WITH YOUR UNDERSTANDING OF THE PROBLEM,
YOU DON'T UNDERSTAND THE PROBLEM.**

There are hundreds of things that **can** be overlooked in any problem definition. If you can't think of even three, all that says is that you can't, or won't, think at all.

Can you think of three things that might be wrong with the manager's solution to the problem of the dangerous tool?

THINK OF THREE REASONS IT WON'T WORK...

8

MISSING THE MISFIT

When some machine goes wrong, we're inclined to blame the person who gets his bottom punched, rather than the person who made the tool. Dan's tool was an exception because it was made for such limited use. Usually, by the time the flaw in the design becomes painfully obvious, the designer is long gone and far away. If the marking punch had been sold widely, instead of made for private use, each injured party would be blamed because "he should have watched where he sat." At best, the person who placed the tool in an upright position would have been blamed for "not thinking of the safety of others." We assume that if the tool is on the market, *thousands* of others must have used it without getting punctured. If they had, they surely would have complained, wouldn't they?

The problem of displacement is compounded by the existence of *designers*—special people whose job it is to solve problems, in advance, for other people. Designers, like landlords, seldom if ever experience the consequences of their actions. In consequence, designers continually produce *misfits. A misfit is a solution that produces a mismatch with the human beings who have to live with the solution.* Some mismatches are downright dangerous.

MISSING THE MISFIT

Long ago, men didn't shave their faces. Later, they somehow perceived a discrepancy between beards and happiness, so they began to shave, or be shaved. Sharpening their razors, they often cut themselves—until the "safety razor" was invented with disposable blades. No shaver ever cut himself sharpening a disposable blade, but lots of shavers' wives or maids cut themselves doing the actual disposal. And, frequently, it was little children who got cut, when they found undisposed disposable blades.

Eventually, medicine cabinets were built with slots for disposing of the used blades. Where there was such a cabinet, the women and children, at least, were relatively safe (until women, for some reason, started shaving their legs and underarms). But for decades the shavers cut their fingers trying to get the blade from the razor to the slot. Millions of men and women, watching their life's blood trickle into the sink and over the clean towels, thought, "Too bad there's no other way to dispose of these blades. If there were, *somebody* would have invented it. It must be that I'm very clumsy and inadequate."

Then, one day, someone did invent something—heaven only knows why. In this new invention, blades were dispensed in packages which received the used blade before dispensing the new one. It wasn't a very complex invention, and many versions quickly followed the original. The problem was recognizing the problem in the first place—or, rather, having the designers recognize it. Perhaps the designers went to barbers for shaves—or perhaps they had beards.

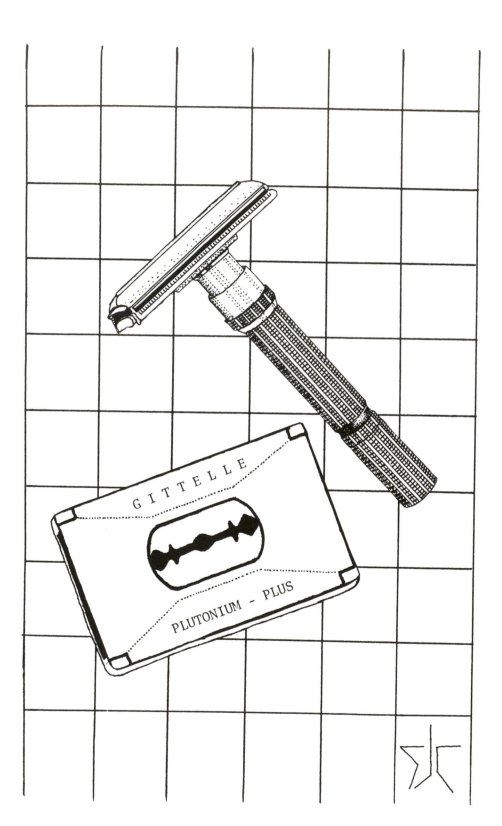

GITTELLE

PLUTONIUM - PLUS

MISSING THE MISFIT

Or perhaps there were no designers, once the basic disposable blade idea was worked out. Who needs a designer, once the problem is solved?

Most misfits are easy to *solve,* once they are *recognized.* Some require action by "the proper authorities," but most can be successfully dispatched by those who have to live with them. Human beings are so adaptable, they'll put up with almost any sort of misfit—until it comes to their consciousness that it doesn't *have* to be that way. Then comes trouble.

When the latest energy "crisis" caused a national lowering of the speed limit in the USA to 55 miles per hour, everybody thought it would be easy to go back to 65 or higher whenever the "crisis" subsided. Unfortunately for various parties with vested interests in higher speed limits, the lower speed limit was accompanied by a drastically lowered accident and death rate. Until this grand "experiment" took place, nobody *knew* for sure why 50,000 people died every year on the highways. Auto manufacturers blamed the drivers; everybody but the alcohol industry blamed drunken driving; but nobody really blamed the legislators for allowing such a high speed limit.

Not all accidents could be attributed to speed limits, but the facts demonstrated that one big slice of them could be. All that had changed in a few months was the public's perception of the misfit of speed limit to car, driver, and road. But what a change! It will take years before the speed limit can gradually slip back up to its previous lethal level. If it rose too fast, somebody might notice the change.

The *sudden* change in the speed limit brought the misfit of highway speed and safety to the foreground of everybody's consciousness. Before this change, speed limits had been creeping upwards for years, along with accident rates, but few people were aware of the association between them. In the same way, any new "solution" is likely to make its users more aware than the original designer of a faulty problem definition. But once the original unfamiliarity has passed, human adaptability makes the misfit invisible. Once again, we see how important is the rule:

DON'T LEAP TO CONCLUSIONS, BUT DON'T IGNORE YOUR FIRST IMPRESSION.

But what can we do long after our first impressions have faded? Must we always call in outsiders—consultants or other "foreigners"—to give us the freshness of view we no longer have? Although there's nothing wrong with consultants (or so say Don and Jerry), we *can* learn techniques for reducing our dependence on their services.

For one thing, to get a fresh point of view, we can call upon almost *anybody* as our "consultant." Try to avoid the "expert" consultant, for he may be even more adapted to the status quo than we are. Try asking the man and woman in the street what they think of a particular design or problem definition. In explaining our approach to the uninitiated, we force ourselves into a fresh view of the matter—and so perceive new misfits.

When we travel to foreign lands, we inevitably experience "new" things as strange and awkward. The money doesn't make sense. The street signs are in the wrong places. The toilet paper is all wrong. An even more useful experience, though, is to *accompany* a foreign traveller through your *own* country, for through the foreigner's eyes you will once again perceive the strangeness and awkwardness of your own culture.

Why do we say "once *again* perceive the strangeness...''? Because we once perceived the strangeness as *children*—until adults hammered into our little heads: "This is not merely the only possible world; it's the best possible world."

Show a Swiss visitor American paper money for the first time. You will inevitably hear, "But they're all the same *size*? How do *blind* people tell them apart?" Your response will be an embarrassed silence, for unless you are blind yourself, you've never thought about money in that way. Never? Well, hardly ever. Not, at least, since you were a child—but then you rarely saw even a dollar bill, so it wasn't much of a problem.

The next response of the Swiss visitor will be, "And they're all the same *color!* Don't people make lots of mistakes in making change?" Again, embarrassed silence as you contemplate how many mistakes comprise a *lot*. Sure, you've had experiences of being shortchanged, or longchanged, when a five was mistaken for a ten. Until this moment, though, you've always accepted this rate of mistakes as a "law of nature." With your new consciousness, you begin to notice all the adaptations Americans make to cut down the number of such errors. For a few days, every cashier you encounter becomes an object of heightened awareness—until you finally fade back into your old, comfortable oblivion. For a real treat to your awareness, try paying with two-dollar bills for a few days.

Such experiences give us a clue how to proceed when trying to perceive misfits:

TEST YOUR DEFINITION ON A FOREIGNER, SOMEONE BLIND, OR A CHILD, OR MAKE YOURSELF FOREIGN, BLIND, OR CHILDLIKE.

ARE YOUR LIGHTS ON?

Take some object that you handle every day—a shoe, a shirt, a fork, a car door, a toothbrush, or any one of a thousand others. Set yourself the exercise of "seeing" it from the point of view of someone from another country who has never seen one before. Then try using it with your eyes tightly closed—or your ears, or nose, as appropriate. Imagine that you are one-fourth your present size and trying to handle this object for the first time. What happens if you cannot read, or your manual dexterity is not well developed?

Let's try the exercise with some book. Don't even consider the contents, but only the mechanical design. Keep trying different points of view until you come up with a *minimum* of ten items that caused you some inconvenience at the time you were reading—an inconvenience that you simply accepted at the time. For instance, Don came up with this list in a few minutes:

1. It was hard to keep the place when I put the book down.

2. Because I couldn't take just part of the book with me, I had to carry the whole book even when I knew I would use only part of it.

3. The binding was too heavy for handling, but too light for long term wear.

4. It wouldn't stay open without holding it open.

5. The pages ripped too easily.

6. Some of the pages were stuck together.

7.   The pages were too glossy, so they reflected an annoying amount of light.

8.   Because the lines on the page were too long, I occasionally returned to the same line, or skipped a line.

9.   The margins were too narrow for making notes.

10. Without a handle of some sort, the book is difficult to carry.

If such an old, established solution can have so many misfits, what hope is there that our untested ideas will be perfect? Not much. We can be fairly confident that

EACH NEW POINT OF VIEW WILL PRODUCE
A NEW MISFIT.

Won't it be better to get these points of view *before* proceeding to implement a "solution," rather than leaving it to a disaster to raise your consciousness?

Each new point of view will pro-duce a new misfit. misfit. misfit MISFIT

9

LANDING ON THE LEVEL

Problem 1: The figure below shows a very familiar object. What is it?

A circle! That's what most people say, without hesitation. Why can they solve this tiny problem so quickly—if in fact they *have* solved it—when other problems take lifetimes to solve, if solved at all? In spite of all the difficulties of getting started—all the perplexities of the preceding chapters—people do solve *this* problem, and thousands of others. Just when we were beginning to believe no problem would ever be solved!

When we solve a problem as fast as most people solve Problem 1, we may not notice *how* we did it. A good way to expose the process is to ask,

HOW COULD WE CHANGE THE PROBLEM STATEMENT TO MAKE THE SOLUTION DIFFERENT?

In this case, the problem statement was a big help. Why? Probably it was the word "familiar." Let's try that hypothesis by changing the problem statement to this:

Problem 2:   The figure shows an object.
              What is it?

Or, we could leave the word "familiar," but remove the emphasis supplied by "very," giving this:

Problem 3:   The figure shows a familiar object.
              What is it?

An even stronger test would be to reverse the sense of the critical word, as in this:

Problem 4:   The figure shows a very unfamiliar object.
              What is it?

The effect of such "trivial" changes in the problem statement can be made the subject of an amusing party game, or scientific experiment. Various people or teams are given slightly different problem statements concerning the same object. In the party game, the answers are then presented to the entire throng, with everyone guessing what the others' problem statements were. In the scientific experiment, the responses can be analyzed to plumb the process by which people establish

WHAT AM I SOLVING?

In our experiments, the overwhelming majority of respondents to Problem 1 will say "circle." The percentage drops when the word "very" is omitted, drops further when the word "familiar" vanishes, and plummets to zero when the original problem is altered by adding the two letters, UN. In the place of the conventional answer, we get such replies as "a hole;" "a hula hoop;" "a pencil, viewed from the eraser end;" "the cross-section of an oblate spheroid;" "a coin made from lutetium;" "the circular lens on the planchet of a Ouija board;" "the central ornament on a Hepplewhite side chair;" "part of the honeycomb of a non-conformist bee;" and "a landing pad for a midget helicopter."

On the other hand, a great many people will refuse to venture any answer to Problem 4, though most will essay something for the other three. When questioned about their non-reply, most participants will say that they felt their chances of "solving" the problem are so slight it's not worth risking an error. We can test this analysis by changing the problem once again, to this:

Problem 5:   The figure shows a very unfamiliar object. Think of the most far-out thing it could be.

With this statement, few people have trouble coming up with some answer. Because we seem to be asking for their **opinion,** rather than the "right" answer, much of the threat is removed. *Everyone* has an opinion—or almost everyone does—and everyone is an expert in his or her personal opinion.

Once we've recognized something as a problem, we usually give it the "once over" in order to place it on a *semantic level.* When the final exam question reads:

Express your views on why Henry the Eighth killed his wives, and of the methods he used for the actual killings.

the student makes a judgment that "express your views" isn't really asking for an opinion, but for the "right" answer. The "real" reasons that Henry the Eighth harbored in his twisted brain are reasons only your professor can fathom with certainty.

Wherever possible, we initially place the problem in the semantic level that lends us the most comfort. If we think our professor is a bleeding-heart liberal, and if we slept through his lecture on Henry the Eighth, we might be most comfortable pretending the question really does ask for our opinion. Later on, we'll take our chances arguing that it's the professor's fault for not being more careful with his wording. If he's a hard-nosed traditionalist, however, we won't pussy-foot with such semantic quibbling. The "most comfortable" level will translate the question into the meaning:

What did I say in the lecture about why Henry the Eighth killed his wives, and about the methods he used for the actual killings.

"Comfort," in this sense, may come because we know how to solve that particular level of problem. It may derive from knowing the source of the problem, the context of the problem, or from a much more subtle feeling about the nature of the problem—a feeling we can't quite articulate, but which we know is "right."

In Problem 1, the word "familiar" ruled out oblate spheroids for most of us, and the quality of the drawing ruled out such things as hula hoops—thus landing the problem in the level of "simple geometry." In Problem 4, the chance that we couldn't *solve* the problem on that level moved some people to bizarre levels of complexity. Yet the same problem threw others into such a state they couldn't establish a semantic level at all.

Had this problem appeared in *Dick and Jane's Golden Book of Puzzles,* we might have been led to the semantic level of "toys"—thus the hula hoop, the spokeless bicycle tire, or the hole in a Tinkertoy wheel. Appearing as it did in this learned, sophisticated problem definition book—a book that has promised to be filled with traps for the unwary—the problem acquired an unbelievably intricate context for establishing the semantic level. Few readers would have considered it a problem in simple geometry. That would have been too obvious. But, then, that would have been a trap for the unwary, wouldn't it?

POSTSCRIPT: *Oh, by the way, if you're now convinced that the figure is a circular representation subject to countless interpretations, try comparing it with some "true" circle. Does this comparison alter your conclusions? Does it make you appreciate the important principle:*

AS YOU WANDER ALONG THE WEARY PATH OF PROBLEM DEFINITION, CHECK BACK HOME ONCE IN A WHILE TO SEE IF YOU HAVEN'T LOST YOUR WAY.

10

MIND YOUR MEANING

"Nothing is too good for our customers." So says the sign in the window, but what does it mean? Is it

>"There is no thing in the world that is too good for our customers."

Or does it mean:

>"Giving them nothing would be giving them something too good for them."

Is this a silly play on words? Doesn't everyone *know* what the sign means? Not likely. Not if our experience with problem statements is any clue. Time and again we've seen well-intentioned problem resolvers trip over words like "nothing," "may," "all," and "or" in what seemed a perfectly clear written statement of a problem.

   In school, of course, we've learned that giving problems with tricky wording is "unfair"—just another way in which the school fails to prepare us for the unfair world outside its ivy-covered walls. Any computer programmer can supply a dozen examples of a misunderstood word, a misplaced comma, or an ambiguous syntax that cost someone $10,000, $100,000, $1,000,000, or just about any price you care to name.

ARE YOUR LIGHTS ON?

In one case, the program's specification read, in part,

"The exception information will be in the XYZ file, too."

The programmer took this to mean,

"*Another* place the exception information appears is the XYZ file."

He assumed, therefore, that the exception information was duplicated somewhere else, so he saw no need for his program to preserve it.

Actually, the writer had meant,

"Another type of information that appears in the XYZ file is the exception information."

Nothing was implied about this information being duplicated elsewhere, and, indeed, it wasn't duplicated. As a result, valuable and unrecoverable information was lost. Before the differing interpretations were discovered, the cost of the lost information had mounted to about $500,000—rather a large bill for one carelessly placed "too."

When half a million dollars flies out the window, heads must surely roll. But *who* should be decapitated? The writer? The programmer? Most English teachers would behead the writer. Problem resolution teachers would put the programmer's neck on the chopping block. Isn't there someone out there who favors a bloodless approach?

MIND YOUR MEANING

We could preach to the writers about the need for clear, understandable problem statements until they drown in an ocean of blah-blah. We could exhort problem resolvers to read more carefully, and they could go blind trying. If past experience is any guide, none of this would help much. No matter how sincere people are, mere *quantity* of effort is not sufficient. You won't ever be sure that *everyone* present has the same understanding of the same words.

We need a social process that tends to get the words off the paper and into their heads. One such process is word play:

ONCE YOU HAVE A PROBLEM STATEMENT IN WORDS, PLAY WITH THE WORDS UNTIL THE STATEMENT IS IN EVERYONE'S HEAD.

Almost any method of play will throw some light on the problem, perhaps revealing a difference in understanding. Consider the simple statement of fact:

Mary had a little lamb.

What could be more clear—until we try some word games. For instance, try placing *emphasis* on one word after another, giving

Mary had a little lamb. (as opposed to *John* having one)

Mary *had* a little lamb. (but doesn't *have* it any more)

Mary had *a* little lamb. (not *several*, as others had)

Mary had a *little* lamb. (not a *big* one, as you thought)

ARE YOUR LIGHTS ON?

Mary had a little *lamb*. (that *dog* belonged to Henry)

You can even stress the words in pairs, triplets, fours, and fives, each combination of which gives a different meaning to the "simple" statement of fact.

Or try the *dictionary approach*. For each word in the sentence, make a list of the dictionary's meanings, then try to apply each of those meanings to the original sentence.

Most often, in the dictionary game, it's the little words that make the difference. Take, for example, HAD. In our *American Heritage Dictionary of the English Language,* we discover that "had" is "the past tense and past participle of have." Already there is cause for grammatical ambiguity, but let's flip forward to page 604, where we find no fewer than 31 definitions of "have". Few ice-cream parlors have more flavors than that!

The first definition fits our preconception of the sentence:

1. To be in possession of, as one's property; own.

The second, however, gives us pause:

2. To be related or in a particular relationship to: *have three children.*

This meaning is the source of an ancient joke:

Mary had a little lamb,
The event made medical history.

MIND YOUR MEANING

As we scan the list, we can create our own jokes, or interpretations, for the following selected definitions:

4. To hold in one's mind; entertain: *have doubts.*

6. To bribe or buy off.

7. To engage the attention of; captivate.

8. To win a victory over; to down.

9. To cheat, deceive, or trick.

10. To possess sexually.

12. To accept or take: *I'll have the gray jacket.*

13. To partake of; consume, as by eating or drinking.

Try the rest yourself. Also try "little," and "lamb." And don't neglect "a" and "Mary" and your next problem statement.

Word games are usually cheaper than unwanted solutions. It behooves us to carry a full quiver of word games to shoot at would-be problem definitions. Here's a list of some other games we've played, each of which has at one time or another saved someone $1,000,000 or more—the Golden List of Word Games:

1. Vary the stress pattern (as in the above example).

2. Change positives to negatives and vice versa.

3. Change MAY to MUST, and MUST to MAY.

4. Change OR to EITHER OR, and vice versa.

5. Change AND to OR, and vice versa.

6. Choose a term that is defined explicitly and substitute the explicit definition in each place the term appears.

7. For each ETC., AND SO FORTH, AND SO ON, etc., add one more explicit example to the list. (Try it with this rule.)

8. Search for *persuasive* words or phrases, such as OBVIOUSLY, THEREFORE, CLEARLY, or CERTAINLY. Replace each such word or phrase with the argument it is supposed to be replacing.

9. Try to draw a picture of what some sentence or paragraph is saying.

10. Express the words in the form of an equation.

11. Express the equation in the form of words.

12. Try to express in words what some picture is trying to say.

13. Replace YOU with WE.

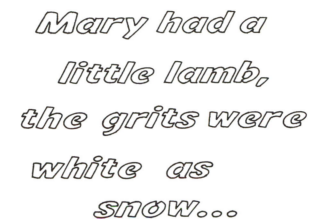

Mary had a little lamb, the grits were white as snow...

14.   Replace WE with YOU.

15.   Replace WE and YOU with BOTH PARTIES.

16.   Replace A with THE and THE with A.

17.   Replace SOME with EVERY.

18.   Replace EVERY with SOME.

19.   Replace ALWAYS with SOMETIME.

20.   Replace SOMETIME with NEVER.

Practice these games on familiar material. Try, for instance, that immortal line:

WHERE THE SKIES ARE NOT CLOUDY ALL DAY.

Then tackle your current problem definition statement. You'll soon see what an important weapon a game can be, so you'll want to add at least 20 *more* games to your personal quiver.

If that number sounds unreasonable, start with the dictionary game, which we'll give you for nothing. In fact, apply the dictionary game to the list of games. Before long, you'll be well on your way to becoming the William Tell of Problem Definition.

PART 4 :

Whose problem is it?

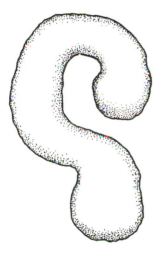

11

SMOKE GETS IN YOUR EYES

A class of 11 students and their brilliant teacher meet every Wednesday afternoon for three hours to discuss problem resolution. Much to their consternation, they discover that although 11 out of the 12 participants don't smoke at all, the twelfth is hooked on cigars.

The classroom is small and not well ventilated. The cigars are cheap and ventilated all too well. After the first hour of the first class, a haze has descended into the breathing space of all but the shortest students. Several of the taller ones are already showing a grayish-green complexion, but the smoker puffs blissful clouds of odoriferous gas into the haze, absolutely unaware of any kind of problem. It is apparent to the teacher, problem resolver that he is, that there is a problem—or soon will be one.

Before reading further, consider the case described above and choose an answer to the following question:

WHOSE PROBLEM IS IT?

(a) the ten nonsmoking students

(b) the smoker

(c) the teacher

(d) the dean of the school

(e)   the college president

(f)   none of the above

(g)   all of the above (including f)

In the actual case, the teacher (c) hardly knew there was a problem because he had passed his formative years in the haze of a cigar-smoking father. He was fully accustomed to foul odors in the air, and almost felt that this filthy habit was perfectly normal. The dean and president, as usual, were completely out of the picture when it came to solving problems, so, by the process of elimination, it had to be either the smoker (b) or the nonsmokers (a).

At the second class meeting, the teacher arrived ten minutes late. Because he had a high rank, the students were forced to wait for him. Seizing the opportunity, one of the nonsmokers began to conduct a problem-solving meeting on the subject of air pollution in the classroom. By the time the teacher arrived, the meeting was in full swing. Even the smoker was cheerfully participating. Perhaps because this was a class in creative problem resolution, the teacher wisely allowed the meeting to continue. Besides, he was outnumbered.

A list of possibilities evolved on the blackboard, including such things as

(1)   All class members would call the smoker at work on the afternoon before class and remind him not to bring cigars.

(2)   A particular class member given to early morning ac-
        tivities would phone the smoker at 4:30am before
        the class to ask why he had smoked during the pre-
        vious class.

(3)   They would let the air out of the smoker's tires—one
        tire for each cigar. It would be an eye for an eye and
        an air for an air...

It took about an hour and a thousand laughs for the smoker
to get the message—but in a way that didn't offend him or
put him in the defensive.

The leader then asked the smoker to suggest which of
the ideas he would find acceptable, or which idea could be
modified to make it acceptable. Very quickly—almost spon-
taneously—he said he would be happy to give up smoking in
the class in favor of other less socially annoying (and maybe
even pleasant) indulgences. In keeping with the creativity
theme of the class, he asked that each student, each week,
create something to nibble on that would be even more orally
gratifying than cigars—or at least more interesting—and which
could be shared by the rest of the class.

The suggestion was cheerfully implemented by all.
The cigar smoking ended forthwith, followed by thousands
of calories of surprising eating—camomile cookies, carrot
cake, barbequed chicken-wing pizza, green tomato pie,
double chocolate fudge with alfalfa sprouts, just to name a
few. The class finished the semester intact, in corpulent bliss.

It's instructive to imagine what the outcome might
have been had the teacher decided that the answer was (c)—
that it was *his* problem. He might have done such things as

(1)   Mandate that there would be *no smoking*, forcing the smoker to drop the class or grind his teeth.

(2)   Mandate that there **would** be smoking, forcing some nonsmokers to leave the class or lose their lunch.

(3)   Mandate alternate smoking and nonsmoking class days, or hours, forcing everybody to be unhappy about the situation.

Instead of mandating anything, he wisely followed one of his own precepts of problem solving:

DON'T SOLVE OTHER PEOPLE'S PROBLEMS WHEN THEY CAN SOLVE THEM PERFECTLY WELL THEMSELVES.

Not only did the interested parties know and feel much more about the problem, but after creating "their" solution, they were ego-involved in seeing that it was carried out. The time they had invested—90 minutes out of a 45-hour semester—gave them another reason for wanting the idea to succeed.

Besides, had the teacher issued exactly the same suggestion *ex cathedra*, it probably wouldn't have been accepted, or, if accepted, not really carried out with enthusiasm. One of our friends, an absent-minded professor of the first rank, frequently discovers, after a meal in an elegant restaurant, that he has forgotten his money. Upon such an occasion, he merely smiles at the proprietor and says, "*We* have a problem." Can you imagine what would happen if he said, "*You* have a problem."? Or even, "*I* have a problem."?

IF IT'S THEIR PROBLEM, MAKE IT THEIR PROBLEM.

12

THE CAMPUS THAT WAS ALL SPACED OUT

A newly established campus of a large state university seems to have a problem that has existed ever since the Lord created automobiles—parking. The campus started out with a surplus of parking lots—indeed, it was pretty much all parking lots. As if to solve the problem of excess parking lots, new buildings were ingeniously constructed over them, one after another. While this overbuilding was taking place, the student body tripled, the faculty doubled, and the administration quintupled. Parking thus became "a problem."

In a move to return power to the people (where we all know it belongs, as long as we're part of the people), the Student-Faculty Senate eliminated all reserved parking except for disabled persons and, of course, the University President. Though there were still sufficient parking locations for anyone coming to campus, most were from one-half to one kilometer from office and classroom buildings.

Another piece of possibly relevant information is the weather, which is rather frequently inclement. Indeed, it has been well and truly said that this campus has but three seasons—snow, mud, and dust.

Before reading further about this case, try to answer the following question: WHOSE PROBLEM IS IT?

(a)   the students

(b)   the faculty

(c)   the University President

(d)   the state legislature

(e)   the governor

(f)   none of the above

(g)   all of the above

By thoughtful elimination, we can determine that (d) and (e) are never the correct answers. (c) might be correct, but the University President has a reserved space, so he cannot be expected to get too upset over the situation. He has the power of decision, all right, for he can and does override the so-called faculty "Senate" whenever they actually try to do anything important. But he never personally experiences the parking problem, so why should he think it is important?

We've already seen how many problems in our society stem from systems designers and decision makers who don't experience the problems they're "responsible" for. The police commissioner of Gotham City has a chauffeur-driven limousine to cart him around town. What does traffic congestion or mugging mean to him? The automotive designers at Mammoth Motors get a new Behemoth IV every time the old ashtrays fill up. What do maintenance costs and troubles mean to them?

The workers in Brontosaurus Tower had hit upon an approach to this situation in trying to arouse their landlord. The principle is simply this:

THE CAMPUS THAT WAS ALL SPACED OUT

IF A PERSON IS IN A POSITION TO DO SOMETHING ABOUT A PROBLEM, BUT DOESN'T HAVE THE PROBLEM, THEN DO SOMETHING SO HE DOES.

Applying this principle to the campus President, the students began parking in his reserved space. Such cars were naturally ticketed and fined, but the students paid the fines collectively, so the cost per person was miniscule.

Unfortunately, the President didn't take this communal action in the proper spirit. He let it be known through official channels that any student parking in *his* space would be summarily dismissed from school. This autocratic action solved *his* problem by making it not *their* problem but, rather, one person's problem at a time. "Divide and conquer" is quite the opposite of the "OUR problem" approach—and thus provides a most useful technique for those who would *prevent* problem resolution. It is the favorite trick of University Presidents and other tyrants.

University students like a challenge. The response to the President's escalation took several weeks to develop, but one day the President's car was found to be resting upon four flat tires. The university police were delegated to fill the tires, but the next day the tires were not only flat, but slashed beyond repair. A 24-hour guard was placed on the President's car, but this occupied the only full-time parking patrolman. Knowing that there was no more ticketing, people started parking anywhere—on lawns, in driveways, even in handicapped spaces.

About this time, some of the faculty members decided to exercise a new and different problem-solving technique—"thinking the unthinkable." In response to "Whose problem is it?" They answered in the first person singular: "It's *my* problem."

THE RESPONSE TO THE PRESIDENT'S ESCALATION TOOK SEVERAL WEEKS TO DEVELOP...

THE CAMPUS THAT WAS ALL SPACED OUT

"MY problem" is not at all the opposite of "OUR problem." Like that approach, it reminds us of possibilities we might otherwise overlook in our haste to establish blame in some other quarter. If, for instance, we keep blaming the "pollution problem" on the "government" or on "big business" or on "people who don't care," we can do little besides writing letters to congresspeople or newspapers. But if we can swallow our pride for just an instant and view the problem as though it were ours alone, we might actually get *something* done about "pollution."

When the professors looked at the parking problem in terms of "It's *my* problem," the problem changed from "There aren't enough parking places" to such things as

(1)   I'm too lazy to walk very far.

(2)   I don't come in early enough to get one of the few good places, because I like to sleep too late.

(3)   I'm not looking for interesting things along the way.

(4)   I wouldn't need to park a bicycle, if I were more fit.

(5)   I'm too interested in being comfortable in bad weather.

(6)   I'm afraid of walking in the dark.

(7)   I need companionship when I go for long walks.

(8)   I don't want to expend very much, if any, energy.

(9)   I'm afraid of falling down on the ice.

(10)   I'll be late for classes if I have to walk too far.

Most of these thoughts lead to the idea of ridding ourselves of the problem by seeing it as a phantom problem and then changing our perceptions of the situation.

Some faculty members were able to decide that exercise would be good for them, which they all knew anyway. Why not combine getting to work *with* exercise, rather than looking at the work and the exercise separately—rushing home to go to the tennis club?

Armed with this rationalization, these learned professors were able to change the problem from "How can I get the *nearest* parking space?" to "How can I get the *farthest* parking space?"—and, *voila,* the problem vanished. By wearing hiking clothes whenever the weather threatened, they overcame their fear of discomfort. Indeed, comfort generally was increased—not just coming from the parking lot—for hiking clothes are designed for comfort rather than for intimidating students with their professorial looks. By taking new routes and looking for new things, they made the walking ever so much more enjoyable. One professor wore a pedometer to measure daily "kilometrage"—thereby developing his instincts for the metric system. Another added to his exercise by bending and stooping to pick up litter along the way—a minimum of ten pieces per trip—thereby doing something about "pollution" at the same time as he flattened his flabby belly.

THE CAMPUS THAT WAS ALL SPACED OUT

Looking back on the countless hours of frustrated searching, speeding, and swearing for the nearest parking space, they wondered why they hadn't resolved the problem sooner. They realized that once they followed a simple rule:

TRY BLAMING YOURSELF FOR A CHANGE
—EVEN FOR A MOMENT.

the problem evaporated.

In truth, we can't honestly say that the problem was solved for the masses. Years later, we still see a lot of red, angry faces circling the campus and burning scarce fossil fuel in quest of *the* perfect spot. Indeed, if the truth be told, very few people actually adopted this approach to solution—so few, in fact, that there's only one or two battered ol' cars sitting in "Outer Mongolia"—the farthest reaches of the parking lot. But at least it's been resolved for one or two battered ol' problem solvers.

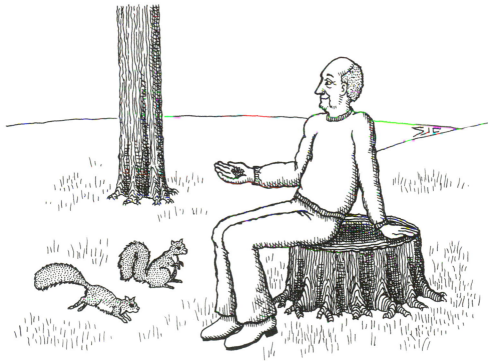

13

THE LIGHTS AT THE END OF THE TUNNEL

A long auto tunnel through the mountains above Lake Geneva has just been completed. Just before the opening, the chief engineer remembers that she has forgotten to warn motorists to turn on their lights before entering the tunnel. Even though the tunnel is well illuminated, the motorists must be prepared to prevent a catastrophe in the event of a power failure—a plausible eventuality in the mountains.

A sign is made saying:

WARNING: TUNNEL AHEAD
PLEASE TURN YOUR HEADLIGHTS ON.

The tunnel, with the sign well ahead of the entrance, is opened on schedule, and everyone relaxes, now that the problem is solved.

About 400 meters past the Eastern end of the tunnel stands the world's most scenic rest stop, with a sweeping view from high above the lake. Hundreds of tourists stop there each day to enjoy the view, perform important bodily functions, and perhaps partake of a small but tasty "pique-nique". And every day, ten or more of those hundreds return to their cars, refreshed in body and soul, only to find a dead battery from having left their lights on! The gendarmes are tying up most of their resources getting them started or hauling them away. Tourists are complaining and swearing to tell their friends not to visit Switzerland.

As usual, we ask you to pause and ask yourself:

WHOSE PROBLEM IS IT?

(a)   the drivers

(b)   the passengers (if any)

(c)   the chief engineer

(d)   the gendarmes

(e)   the president of the canton

(f)   the automobile clubs

(g)   none of the above

(h)   all of the above

The strong tendency in this type of problem—with an explicit "designer" or "engineer"—is to consider that it is *her* problem. Not only do the drivers in this case consider it the engineer's problem, but the engineer probably does too. It's a common impression among architects, engineers, and other designers that *they* must take care of everything.

In this instance, the engineer considered various solutions she could impose upon the drivers and their passengers.

(1)   She could put a sign at the end of the tunnel saying, TURN OFF YOUR LIGHTS but then people would turn off their lights at night...

(2)   She could ignore the situation and let people...No, that was already happening, and the government officials think the engineer has done a lousy job.

THE LIGHTS AT THE END OF THE TUNNEL

(3)   She could put a battery-charging station at the scenic overlook. But that would be expensive to maintain, and would make people even more furious if it didn't work.

(4)   She could give the recharging station franchise to a private firm. But that would commercialize the overlook and be unacceptable to the government and the tourists.

(5)   She could put a more explicit sign at the end of the tunnel.

The engineer felt intuitively that there should be some way to write a more explicit sign. She worked on several alternatives and eventually came up with a masterpiece of Swiss precision:

**IF IT IS DAYLIGHT, AND IF YOUR LIGHTS ARE ON,
TURN OFF YOUR LIGHTS;**

**IF IT IS DARK, AND IF YOUR LIGHTS ARE OFF,
TURN YOUR LIGHTS ON;**

**IF IT IS DAYLIGHT, AND IF YOUR LIGHTS ARE OFF,
LEAVE YOUR LIGHTS OFF;**

**IF IT IS DARK, AND IF YOUR LIGHTS ARE ON,
LEAVE YOUR LIGHTS ON.**

ARE YOUR LIGHTS ON?

By the time anybody had finished reading this sign, his car would be over the guardrail and gurgling to the bottom of the lake, which wouldn't be an acceptable solution at all. Besides, what about funerals? There must be a better way!

Instead of all this complication, the chief engineer took the approach of "It's THEIR problem"—with a tiny *assist* from the engineer. She assumed that the drivers had a strong motivation to solve the problem, but might need a little reminding. She also assumed that the drivers—if they were to be licensed at all—couldn't be such complete dummies. All they needed was a sign at the end of the tunnel reading:

ARE YOUR LIGHTS ON?

THE LIGHTS AT THE END OF THE TUNNEL

If they weren't smart enough to deal with *that*, dead batteries were the least of their problems.

This sign eliminated the problem, and the message was short enough that it could be put on the sign in several languages. The engineer always remembered her lesson from this situation:

IF PEOPLE REALLY HAVE THEIR LIGHTS ON,
A LITTLE REMINDER MAY BE MORE EFFECTIVE
THAN YOUR COMPLICATED SOLUTION.

Are *your* lights on?

PART 5 :

Where does it come from ?

14

JANET JAWORSKI JOGGLES A JERK

During a thaw in the Cold War, Janet Jaworski decided to use her life's savings for a visit to her grandmother in Poland. Step by step she wended her way through the forest of paperwork needed to get a visa—five separate forms, three different trips to a notary public interspersed with waiting periods of from 3 days to 6 weeks, four long distance calls at her expense, nine letters, and two translator's fees. Several times, Janet almost gave up. But she knew her grandmother was 84 years old. She might not live long enough for Janet to meet her if the process had to be started over from scratch.

Finally, visa in hand, she flew to Zurich, then on to Warsaw. After standing in three different lines to have her papers inspected, she found herself shunted to the gray office of a gray-skinned bureaucrat in a gray suit exactly matching the rest of the decor. For what seemed like five minutes, he fingered through some files in his drawer as if he had not seen her enter the room. Then, as if struck with an inspiration, he turned to the papers which had been laid on his desk by the attendant. After several rather disapproving glances at her visa photos and her face he asked, "Mrs. Jaworski?"

"*Miss* Jaworski," Janet replied with all the politeness and friendliness she could muster.

Mr. Grayface cleared his throat as if to register his moral feelings about unmarried ladies traveling unescorted, then scanned her papers line by line with his index finger. "Oh, yes, *Miss* Jaworski." He pushed his chair back a few inches and placed his palms on the edge of his desk. "Just *what* is the purpose of your visit to Poland, *Miss* Jaworski?"

"I've come to visit my grandmother in Ostroda. It says there on that form."

"Yes, I see that Miss Jaworski. However, since your papers are not in order, I wanted to confirm that there was no mistake."

Janet's fingertips began to tingle. If the feeling moved up her arms, she would be in full panic. "Not in order? What's not in order?"

"As you can plainly see," he gestured with his open hand, releasing the edge of the desk for just an instant, "there are supposed to be *eight* notarized copies of each page. And," he gestured with the other hand, "there are just as plainly only *seven*."

Mr. Grayface now returned both palms to the edge of the desk and leaned back a few centimeters as if to suggest that the next move was up to Janet. She forced the tingle back down from her wrists to her knuckles. She knew she had a problem—one she would never solve in a panic. Having been brought up in the United States, Janet wasn't familiar with Polish bureaucrats. Though she suspected that there was a higher culture encompassing all the world's bureaucrats, she knew that was just a guess. She desperately needed some time to think about her problem and to get more information, so she said as calmly as she could, "My goodness, what *can* have happened to the other one. I know it was there when I received the visa. Perhaps it is still in my luggage, or could your assistant have lost it on the way over here?"

ARE YOUR LIGHTS ON?

Mr. Grayface snapped some instructions in Polish to the attendant, who was lingering by the door. Janet hadn't noticed the attendant, but now she realized that his presence was a potential clue to the source of her problem. Mr. Grayface might have been seeking a bribe, but hardly would have done so with the attendant in the room. Of course, the attendant might not have spoken English, more than the few words they had exchanged. Perhaps he was in on the bribery, but all things considered, it now seemed less likely that the problem came from that angle. Well, Janet thought, just where *did* the problem come from?

Under the circumstances, it was tempting to put the entire problem down to "bureaucracy," which is another way of shrugging your shoulders and saying, "That's just the way things are. It's *nature*, or *human nature*, and there's nothing to be done about it."

Problems that come from "Nature" are the worst kind, for two reasons. First, we feel helpless to do anything about a problem that seems to come from so remote a source. Indeed, we often ascribe a problem to Nature so as to evade responsibility for doing anything about it. "It's only human nature to overeat, to crave what you can't have, and to pad your expense account."

The second reason is Nature's indifference. Whenever we can impute a problem to a *human* source, or to a *real* object or action, we have a toehold on a possible solution. By getting at the source, or understanding the source's motivation for creating the problem, we may obliterate the problem or see what will alleviate it. But *Nature,* by her very nature, has *no* motivation. As Einstein said, "Nature is crafty, but not malicious." Because she is entirely indifferent to us and our problems, she gives us the toughest problems of all.

JANET JAWORSKI JOGGLES A JERK

Janet, faced with her visa problem, recognized her inclination to impute the whole mess to "bureaucracy." Had she yielded to that temptation, she would have been placing her entire trip—her life's savings—in the hand of "Fate," which is another name for "Nature"—the world's number one excuse for inactivity. Unwilling to accept such a magnificent risk, Janet posed the crucial question:

WHERE DOES THIS PROBLEM COME FROM?

With this starting point, she was able to construct a variety of candidates, such as

(1)   The attendant actually had lost the eighth copy.

(2)   She actually misplaced it, or never had it.

(3)   Mr. Grayface was an incompetent bureaucrat.

(4)   Mr. Grayface was a competent bureaucrat, but with some other goal than to get her into Poland to see her grandmother.

(5)   Mr. Grayface didn't have the authority to do anything about such an exception, so the problem came from his superior, at some level.

Janet could see that the list might grow even longer, but at least she'd removed the problem from the realm of the "natural" and placed it in the realm of constructive thought, and possible decisive action.

15

MISTER MATCZYSZYN MENDS THE MATTER

In the modern urban world, we rarely face Nature in the raw. We can pass the entire working day without knowing, much less caring, whether or not the sun is shining. For the urban worker, the bureaucracy itself is Nature. We can hardly pass an hour without knowing *and* caring whether or not the Big Boss is radiating his smiling countenance upon the organization.

Under such circumstances, it is all too easy to begin thinking of the bureaucracy as a "natural" phenomenon—like sunshine warming the cool sand, or like maggots devouring a rotting fish. Yet bureaucracies always begin with some process of *selection*—a process which is never quite "natural" selection. Recently, we've been given the Peter Principle, which says that bureaucrats rise in an organization until they reach their level of incompetence. More recently, we've received the Paul Principle, which says that in modern organizations, the difficulty of the job rises until it leaves each bureaucrat above his level of competence. Though these selection processes exist, they are but a few of the many that act to place particular people on particular rungs of the ladder of organizational power.

Observers since antiquity have noted these processes at work, always with a slight or not-so-slight moral tone to the observation. A good example is Robert Burns' poem, *The Dean of the Faculty*, in which he recounts the process by which, then as now, the luminaries of the university are chosen by their peers. In one stanza, Burns moralizes at the faculty:

> **With your honours, as with a certain king,**
> **In your servants this is striking,**
> **The more incapacity they bring,**
> **The more they're to your liking.**

In other words, if the candidate lacks the capacity for the job, he will be all the more beholden to those who appointed him. While this thought might not have comforted Janet, it did give her a clue about where to start.

The bureaucratic robot sitting silently across the desk waiting for the baggage to be delivered had no doubt been chosen—like university deans, bank vice-presidents, and other middle-level bureaucrats—for incompetence. He is both beholden to the bosses for his job and no challenge whatsoever to their jobs. "Can it really be possible," Janet considered, "that Mr. Grayface is really *incapable* of dealing with such a trivial problem as a missing copy? In that case, I shall have to go over his head."

"But perhaps the problem lies with his superior?" Janet understood that another selection process might be at work—superiors select subordinates who can keep the clients from moving up the chain of command. If a subordinate cannot stop the clients, then the superior will have to interrupt whatever it is he does, in order to deal with the problem personally. "In that case," Janet reasoned, "Mr. Grayface has been specifically *chosen* for his ability to be somewhat dense and intractable."

111

Yet Mr. Grayface was also a bit discourteous, at least to Janet's American view of courtesy. If a bureaucrat acts with discourtesy, it may be wise to extend our question further:

WHERE DOES THE DISCOURTESY COME FROM?

"He could be trying to frighten me so I won't go over his head. On the other hand, he's taking the risk that I might take offense and insist on reporting his discourtesy to his superior." Janet recalled reading somewhere that most functionaries become annoyed—and thus discourteous—when they **lack the authority** to make such momentous decisions as allowing your visa to pass with a mere seven copies. They are discourteous because you have reminded them of their servile position in life—their inability to meet your quite reasonable request.

Janet thought about going over Mr. Grayface's head. At this point in her thinking, it seemed that regardless of the source of the problem, it would be best to attempt getting to a higher level. She would just smile politely, then firmly request to see the next person up the line. This approach could get her admitted to Poland forthwith—because of Mr. Grayface's fear of disturbing the boss. If not, it would eventually get her into the country once she reached the person actually in charge, who isn't necessarily polite or stupid. Because the eighth copy couldn't possibly make a difference that a copying machine couldn't cure, Janet figured that her problem would be solved as soon as she could reach that point in the bureaucracy where there was a modicum of intelligence.

MISTER MATCZYSZYN MENDS THE MATTER

But what if there wasn't any intelligence *anywhere* in the chain of command? Is it really possible that all of those Polish jokes are true? How bad could things be? Could Mr. Grayface really be so stupid that he couldn't resolve the problem of the eighth copy?

"Perhaps I'm not being fair to the bureaucrats. Not all the selection is done by the higher-ups. After all, Mr. Grayface spends a lot more of his time with tourists like me than with his boss. The way *they* treat him is bound to have an effect. If he's intransigent in the face of my problems and demands, perhaps that arises from thousands of other tourists who have treated him rudely, like a gray, robotic functionary. Perhaps *I'm* the source of the problem?"

"For a start," Janet decided, "I'll stop thinking of him as Mr. Grayface. Let's see, suppose I call him Mr. Warmperson. Or, better yet, suppose I find out his name! I've complained so many times about being treated as a nameless person, or as a number, but how often have I neglected to ask the name of the clerk who was serving me?"

Janet pulled her chair forward toward the desk and, in so doing, realized that she had been seated in a defiant posture. "Mr.... Oh, I'm sorry, I didn't get your name. Even though my family came to America from Poland, I'm not very good with Polish names."

Mr. Warmperson looked up from his papers, his face relaxed a bit from surprise. "Mr. Matczyszyn, Miss Jaworski. Jan Matczyszyn."

His shoulder came forward with a suggestion that he would like to shake hands, and Janet remembered what her father had told her about introductions in Europe. She extended her hand across the desk, saying, "I'm pleased to meet you Jan. Please call me Janet.

MISTER MATCZYSZYN MENDS THE MATTER

In shaking her hand, Jan Matczyszyn gave his first smile, which made Janet wonder whether Matczyszyn didn't mean Warmface in Polish. The smile definitely encouraged her to continue the conversation. "My grandfather was named Jan," she beamed, "and I was named after him. He died before my father came to America after the war, and my father never saw him again."

"Ah, your father was born in Poland?"

"Oh, yes. He was in the Armed Forces in exile—a pilot. While taking his flight training in Nebraska, he met my mother, whose family came from Poland in the nineteenth century. That's why he never came back after the war."

"How interesting. My brother was in the Air Force, too, though he wasn't as fortunate as your father. He was shot down by the Nazis, leaving me as the only son. I was, myself, too young for the war—I wanted very much to have a chance to avenge my brother's death."

"Perhaps my father knew your brother. I'll have to write him about it..."

There's no need for us to continue this conversation, which is of most interest to Jan, Janet, and her father. Any reader could predict how the affair of the eighth copy will come out—and did in fact come out. Approaching public servants with courtesy and respect for their humanity and competence will, for the most part, evoke humanity and competence. In a country like Switzerland, where this kind of thing has been going on since they gave up fighting other people's wars, it even seems *natural.* A bank teller will help you fill out your withdrawal slip correctly. A salesperson will actually take you around the corner to a place that carries an item that's out of stock. And, as happened to Janet in Poland, the visa officer will lend you a coin from his own pocket to run the copier for that eighth facsimile. It all follows naturally once you determine *where the problem actually comes from,* especially since

THE SOURCE OF THE PROBLEM
IS MOST OFTEN
WITHIN YOU.

POSTSCRIPT: *This has to be one of the most disappoint-
ing chapters in this book, so we've added a postscript to
cheer you up.   What a crushing blow to discover that the
villain was the hero and the hero—you—was the villain. We're
sorry, but we had to do it to you, at least once. Based on
Don and Jerry's experience, the problem actually comes from
the problem solver 53.27% of the time, which certainly justi-
fies having one moralizing chapter on the subject. Now that
the morality is disposed of, you can go back to reading about
how stupid other people are—a guaranteed road to moral uplift and well-being of the soul.*

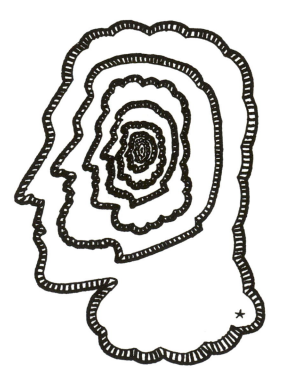

16

MAKE-WORKS AND TAKE-CREDITS

Not all bureaucratic problems can be solved with a smile. For one thing, they often come clad in writing, and how can one smile in a memorandum? For instance, imagine that you work in an institution which habitually circulates memoranda such as the following:

TO: All Staff and Ships at Sea

FROM: His Eminence, The Dean

SUBJECT: Utilization of Commas in Weekly Punctuation
Reports

It has recently come to my attention that the utilization of commas in the weekly report concerning the quantity of punctuation employed by each member of the staff has been confusing to certain members of the Board. According to my analysis, the problem seems to lie in the inability of certain members of the staff to distinguish between commas utilized in the text for purposes of punctuation and commas utilized in the text for purposes of reporting upon the utilization of commas in texts.

I would suggest a solution along these lines, with details to be worked out by a Committee on Commas which I shall presently appoint:

1. Commas utilized for purposes of punctuation should be left as normally used in English or American texts.

2. Commas reporting upon the utilization of commas in other texts, or in their own texts, should be enclosed within single quote marks, like this: ' , '.

2a. As a potential alternative to part 2 of this solution, the commas reporting upon utilization of commas in other texts, or in their own texts, should be enclosed within *double* quote marks, like this: " , ".

I am circulating this memo to the distribution list in order to obtain the fullest possible feedback from the entire staff concerned with this pressing problem, so that we all may input our creative and innovative ideas.

As this phenomenal memorandum circulates, there will be an abundance of smiles, none of which is likely to be given to the face of His Eminence. What is to be done? Can we get a clue from asking, once again:

WHERE DOES THE PROBLEM COME FROM?

Whenever we find a vast circulation of bureaucratic activity, full of sound and fury, signifying nothing, we may be facing a problem that comes from **nowhere**. Or, more precisely, that comes **from the problem itself**. A classic example of this sort of self-perpetuating problem is the International Conference.

MAKE-WORKS AND TAKE-CREDITS

While writing this book, we had the pleasure of reading about yet another International Disarmament Conference taking place in Geneva—a place where the International Conference has been developed to a high art form. Could it be, the Geneva resident speculates, that disarmament *problems* are so intractable because disarmament *conferences* are so attractive?

What would happen to the Arms Race if the disarmament conferees began working at 6:30 in the morning, like honest Swiss workingmen and workingwomen do? Or if the chairs were hard wood instead of soft leather? Or if the meals were frozen fish sticks and soggy potato chips at an Akron drive-in, rather than *omble chevalier* and *pommes anglaises* at Geneva's *Le Senat*?

Now don't get us wrong. We have nothing against disarmament. Nor do we demean the distinguished ladies and gentlemen whose arduous labors for the welfare of the poor, tired, huddled masses must occasionally be relieved by a spot of gaiety and pleasure. We merely wish to indicate the bare possibility of the problem-solving *process, person,* or *institution* becoming the problem itself.

In the old days, when radicals were really radical, they used to say, "If you're not part of the solution, you're part of the problem." It could well be different: "If you're part of today's solution, then you're part of tomorrow's problem." Come to think of it, what *did* happen to those old radicals—they definitely *were* part of the solution.

Speculate with us for a moment, just for speculation's sake. What would happen, after all, if the Nations of the World suddenly disarmed? Would the *patisseries* in Geneva suffer reversals, and half the bureaucrats find themselves transported—tourist class—to the Akrons of the world? Not bloody likely!

ARE YOUR LIGHTS ON?

Recent history is strewn with examples of famous problem-solving institutions whose problems have disappeared. *They* didn't pack their formal wear and catch the next Swissair flight home. No, indeed! Instead, they sought *another* problem to solve. The veritable end of polio didn't see the March of Dimes come to a Halt. There were plenty of other worthy diseases to conquer. The end of the War (any war) didn't see the march of the armies come to a halt, either. True, they became "standing" armies, but that doesn't mean they stood around doing nothing. More often than not, a standing army finds domestic problems urgently claiming their peculiar talents.

In short, the *ultimate* source of the problem may be nowhere at all. In other words,

IN THE VALLEY OF THE PROBLEM SOLVERS, THE PROBLEM CREATOR IS KING, OR PRESIDENT, OR DEAN.

Which brings us back to our original problem—how to handle the memo concerning commas?

Your father's father may have told you,

> **"There's two kinds of people in the world, those that do work and those that make work for others to do. Keep away from the makeworkers and you'll do all right."**

Or, your mother's father may have said,

There's two kinds of people in the world, those that do work and those that make work for others to do.

ARE YOUR LIGHTS ON?

"There's two kinds of people in the world, those that *do work* and those who *take credit*. Keep in the first group—there's much less competition there."

Either of these remarkable observations can be used to solve the memorandum problem. One way is to be physically separated from the people who generate memoranda. Such a separation is most readily accomplished by creating one small group of elegantly decorated offices—preferably on the top floor of the tallest available building—far from the drab work areas. How will you get administrators to move to them? How do you get bees to come to a pansy patch? Flies to a dung heap? Without any fuss, the administrators will wind up in the top of the tower at their Herman Miller desks, leaving the workers in the basement—at their orange crates—doing the work.

In grandfather's day, the age of xerography had not yet dawned. In that simpler time, physical separation was sufficient to keep the administrators feeding their makework to one another. In this more advanced age, when any fool with the key to the copier can become a widely-read author, separation is not enough. Sooner or later, the workers will have to come to grips with that indispensable problem-creator, the memorandum.

We have received the *Utilization of Commas* memo and don't know what to do. Knowing that the problem comes from nothing, we ask ourselves, "What would grandpa have done?" Taking a firm grip on our ball-point pen, we scribble across the upper right-hand corner,

"A fascinating concept. Let's discuss."

and route the original paper back to His Eminence. (Don't clutter your files with a copy—let the Circulation Department be your filing system.)

At least three or four feedback cycles should pass before His Eminence realizes that he cannot get a meeting together merely by having his secretary phone everybody for an open time. When he finally *decrees* a meeting, be sure to have a dental appointment at the same time. (Keep a cavity in reserve, unfilled.) Then, after the meeting, take the announcement memo and scribble across the upper right-hand corner:

> *"Sorry I couldn't make it—dentist!!*
> *What about semicolons? Let's discuss."*

With any imagination at all, you should free one month from administrative interference each time His Eminence sends you a memo. You use almost no effort, no filing space, no clerical time, and—what is most important to our feathered friends of the forest—no paper other than what is sent to you. By sending the problem right back where it came from, you give all the credit to the dean, but you may get some work done.

Are you afraid to try it? Don't be, for there's really no chance of the makeworkers figuring out what you're doing. In fact, they'll love every minute of it.

17

EXAMINATIONS AND OTHER PUZZLES

Nowadays, most schoolchildren know where babies come from. On the other hand, they seem to think that exam problems are delivered to the earth by storks. Or perhaps they think that it's "dirty" to talk about *where problems come from*? Too bad for them, because the *source* of a problem often contains some key element in its resolution.

Consider the typical homework problems on which young minds are fattened for ultimate slaughter in final examinations. Clever students soon learn that the assigned homework almost *always* has something to do with the material covered in class the preceding week. In other words, you don't need to resort to the Laws of Thermodynamics—this week is Light and Optics. And woebetide the professor who slips in a tricky problem taken from two weeks previous. The students soon cure him of that perversion—and the homework system is perpetuated.

In the end, then, it's the students themselves who reinforce this homework pattern. Although it simplifies each week's work, it crushes them when it comes time for the final exam. At this fatal instant, the page is covered with problems that might come from *any one of fifteen weeks*. Gone with the wind is the one clue upon which they have learned most to depend—where the problem came from!

ARE YOUR LIGHTS ON?

How amusing that students complain that school doesn't prepare them for the "real world"—whatever that is—and fail to notice that it doesn't even prepare them for the world of final examinations!

But examinations don't come from storks, either. The *clever* student "reads" the exam with an eye to its progenitor. If you don't give the professor the answer he wants, you're a fool.

For instance, when taking the "comprehensive" examinations for the PhD, you'd better not make the mistake of thinking it's really "comprehensive." It comes from the tiny brains of a small number of very narrow-minded faculty. The first essential step is to deduce which professor in the department wrote the question and will therefore be reading it. Without the step of asking,

WHERE DOES THE PROBLEM COME FROM?

you might make the mistake of praising the Romans instead of the Greeks, Burns instead of Browning, or transubstantiation instead of consubstantiation.

Because an exam is an exam and not a problem generated in outer space, it gives many general clues to solving its problems. Clearly, no problem should take more than the length of the scheduled exam period to figure out. If your method promises to stretch out beyond the appointed hour, it must be dropped, regardless of its elegance.

And, when multiple choice questions are the order of the day, the quicker-witted can sometimes complete the entire exam without ever resorting to problem solving on the intended level. In studying a series of "programmer aptitude tests," we found that *every one* of the "arithmetic skills"

126

questions could be answered without resort to the horrors of arithmetic! Indeed, they could be "solved" without resorting to the *questions*!

Try it for yourself. A typical set of answers was:

(a)   31938

(b)   31929

(c)   31928

(d)   32928

(e)   31828

We know that these answers were constructed by *someone*, not by the stork. That someone would like us to miss the question if we are off by a little bit, so we need only study the structure of the answers to know that choice (c) is "correct." Why? Just try it!

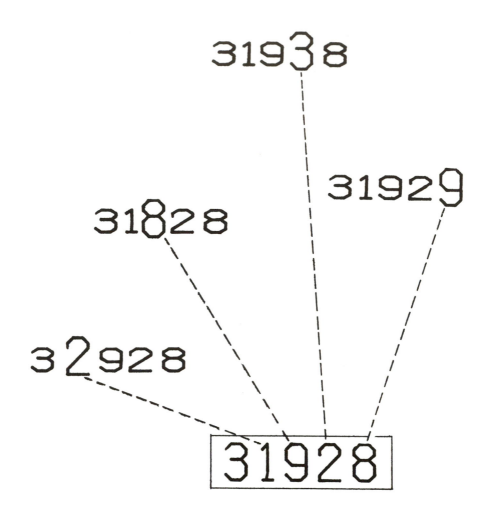

With answers like these, who needs questions? The question is merely a time-wasting distraction—which we may niftily sidestep by asking:

WHO SENT THIS PROBLEM?
WHAT'S HE TRYING TO DO TO ME?

Much of what has traditionally been called "problem-solving" is, in reality, *puzzle solving.* A puzzle is *difficult by design*—but that difficulty implies a *designer.* But we know that the designer wouldn't have selected this puzzle for presentation *if it didn't have some unusual difficulty.*

EXAMINATIONS AND OTHER PUZZLES

This very attempt to make it difficult may give us the clue that, ironically, may prove the first search step we need.

Consider the "chess problem." Chess problems—really puzzles—are *never* cracked by making an "obvious" move—such as putting the king in check. When people get involved in the world of chess puzzles, they unconsciously apply the question, "Where did it come from?" This eliminates "obvious" moves, because the problem must be "hard" to be a good problem. So, how do you fool a chess puzzler? You give him some "problem" that can be, as they say in the trade, "cooked". Because he "knows" it is a puzzle, not a problem, he may take an exceptionally long time before even examining the "obvious" move that cooks the problem. When he finally does, he will be quite angry with you—just like the students whose professor gives a problem from the penultimate chapter.

To one immersed in a puzzle-solving frame of mind, the *obvious* solution is a blow on the head. In military communications, one of the easiest ways to confound an adversary is to send a message in "plain text". The cryptanalysts simply can't take it at face value, knowing the source. Yet generally speaking, all sorts of military problems are simpler than many day-to-day civilian problems—simply because there is a known "opponent" whose characteristics, properly applied, greatly reduce the number of definitions to be considered.

PART 6 :

Do we _really_ want to solve it ?

18

TOM TIRELESS TINKERS WITH TOYS

By now we know that most people, most of the time, feel that they have some sort of problem. By our broad definition of "problem," these people *must* be correct, for a problem is a difference between someone's desires and the way things seem to be.

Knowing that you have a problem is a matter of feeling. If you feel you have a problem, you do have a problem. Knowing *what* that problem is—well, that could be another matter. To be sure, most people with problems also think they know what these problems are. In this, however, they are usually wrong.

A cleverly paradoxical example of such a mistaken impression is the belief that "problem solving" is a big problem. Many people have told us, "My major problem is that I'm not a very good problem solver." Pish-posh! More often than not, *solving,* or *resolving,* a problem is a rather trivial exercise—once we know what the problem is. Possibly the reason schools turn out such poor problem solvers is that students are never given the chance to find out what the problem is—the problem is whatever the teacher *says* it is. You'd better believe it!

Most of us have had schooling—too much of it. We've developed an instinct that makes us seize upon the first statement that looks like a "problem". Then we "solve" it as *fast* as we can, for everybody knows that, on exams, speed counts.

And concentration. So, we've learned problem habits that are pretty hard to overcome when we're not in school, taking exams.

And don't mistake what we're saying. The approach of grabbing the first problem statement, digging in fast, and sticking with it to the bitter end is precisely what you want—when you're trapped in a school system and trying to make the best of a bad business. And even in a few other situations. In fact, the Brontosaurus Tower problem might have been resolved in a trice, had someone leapt to the conclusion that "the elevators are too slow and need to be fixed." The "two-foot blind leap approach" works just often enough to keep it alive. If it *never* worked, people would eventually stop using it—when they'd been out of school long enough.

Another reason the "two-foot blind leap approach" persists is that "problem solving" can be such fun. Once we get going on a smashing problem, only a pervert would want to get in our way. We all know the type: one of those spoil-sports who actually gave up smoking when the Surgeon General's report was issued; who thinks all others should follow his lead; and who never loses an opportunity to preach to them about it. Why, even if what we're solving isn't the "real" problem, it becomes the real problem to us because *we* want to solve it—the more heroically the better. In other words, leave us alone! Who gave Don and Jerry the moral right to interfere with other people's problem-solving fun?

It's a good question, and one we'd better face, because Don and Jerry are two of the world's foremost problem-solving spoilsports. Our moral right comes from the admonition,

DO UNTO OTHERS AS OTHERS HAVE DONE
UNTO YOU.

The two-foot blind leap approach.

ARE YOUR LIGHTS ON?

Each of us, and many of you, have had our fun spoiled by some eager young problem solver disturbing our peaceful equilibrium—that gives us the right to spoil some of the problem solver's fun.

What do we mean by disturbing our peaceful equilibrium? A good example can be drawn from the computer field. When computers first began to be abundant, people did not exactly beat a path to their inventor's door. To an alarming extent, computers were pushed on an unwilling, or at least cautious, public—promoted by an enthusiastic corps of problem solvers specializing in the application of computers to just about anything.

They were young, these problem solvers, with all the impetuousity of youth. Their slogans reflected their youth:

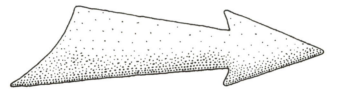

Computers have that effect on youth—or, rather, youth has that effect on computers.

Why, even with several decades of accumulated wisdom to say it isn't so, each new school of hatchlings spilling out of their first programming course is ready to move the earth—given only enough computer time and a terminal to sit at. After all, what has youth ever cared for musty, dusty accumulated wisdom?

And, after all, aren't they right? If nothing else, these young computniks will acquire one valuable lesson from

their unrelenting quest for problems to fit their solution—
"solution probleming," we call it. As they quest, so shall
they learn. Mostly, they'll learn about problem definition.

They will learn how hard it is for people to state their
problems clearly enough to satisfy the precise demands of the
computer, for whom the most trivial steps must be spelled
out in pettifogging detail. At first, these hatchlings will decide that people are no darned good at communicating—and,
at times, this pessimistic assessment will be correct. But
more often than not, communication won't be the source of
the difficulty. We can't communicate what we don't know—
or don't want to know.

But enough of moralizing. What about an example?
Once upon a time, the enthusiastic young programmer, Tom
Tireless, happened upon a toy factory. His effervescence
easily floated him past the outer defensive rings surrounding
the executive suite. Soon, he found himself seated in an
elegant conference room with three vice-presidents. In a few
minutes, Tom had them greedily counting the blessings about
to be showered upon them by his computer.

After some preliminary education of these novices in
the powers of his magical device, Tom, our solution-problemer, asked the vice-presidents if they had any problems lying
about that might prove suitable. Yes, as it happened, they
did have a most pressing problem. It seems that Tanglelang
Toys (TT) had three factories—this one on the Pacific Coast,
another one on the Atlantic Coast, and a third on the coast
of the Missouri River, at Kansas City. From these factories,
they shipped toys to about 50 wholesalers, scattered through-
out the country more or less as shown on this map:

Tanglelang Toys

Factories and wholesalers

Naturally, the executives explained, shipping costs money, thereby adding to the effective cost of each Tanglelang Toy. Moreover, because different wholesalers varied in their shipping distance from the different factories, all shipping costs were different. By this time in the explanation, Tom Tireless was getting restless. He wasn't used to sitting for very long, except at a computer terminal. Certainly not sitting and *listening*.

Tom had long since recognized what their problem was going to be—a classical problem in operations research, one that could be handled niftily on his computer. While they dragged out their explanation, Tom tuned out. He was solving the following problem:

Given a set of orders from their wholesalers, how should TT allocate these orders among the three factories so as to minimize the total cost of doing so—manufacturing plus shipping costs.

By the time the vice-presidents finished explaining that this was indeed their problem, Tom was ready to request the information the computer would need: the total set of orders, the cost of making each toy at each factory, and the cost of shipping each toy from each factory to each wholesaler.

It took the TT executives some time to obtain this information for Tom, but two weeks later it lay neatly assembled on his desk back at the computing center.

Tom spent some time checking the figures this way and that. He began to notice a disturbing pattern. When he finished, he telephoned the executives for an appointment.

"I'm sorry to report," Tom announced, "that I have discovered something curious about your problem. If your figures are correct, then it is possible, for example, to make a teddy bear in this factory and ship it to the Kansas City factory for *less than the cost of making it in Kansas City!* Their cost is $3.95 and yours is $3.07. If you add $.23 for shipping, that makes $3.30, or 65 cents less than their manufacturing cost alone."

Tom laid both hands on the conference table for emphasis. The three vice-presidents sighed and exchanged glances. "Yes," replied the most senior of the three, "we know that ."

"And do you also know that the same hold true for the Atlantic Coast plant?" He paused to let his words sink in. "That you can ship the teddy bear there for $3.38—and they can't make it for less than $4.24?"

"Yes, we're aware of that too. Just what are you driving at, young man?"

"Please, one more question. Are you further aware that *this same pattern holds true for every one of the 374 toys in your line?*"

"But of course we're aware of that. This factory is the most modern in the world—far more efficient than the other two, with lower labor costs, to boot. That's why we built it here."

Tom was perplexed at their density. "But don't you see? You don't need a computer to show you how to reduce your cost to the lowest possible level." It was painful for Tom to admit this, but he continued. "All you have to do is board up the other two plants! Make all your orders here, and ship them from here! Why, even if you didn't ship directly to the wholesalers, but first sent to the shipping docks of your other factories, it would have to be cheaper than the way you're doing it now."

"That's true. But we can't accept that solution."

"What? A solution is a solution. Why can't you accept it?"

"Because the President of TT lives near our Atlantic Plant. And the Chairman of the Board lives in Kansas City. Why, they wouldn't move to the Pacific Coast for anything."

"They certainly wouldn't," the others agreed in unison.

"But then your problem is not one of minimizing costs, but of making your President and Chairman happy?"

Our solution-problemer was exasperated. "Then why did you give the problem to me?"

After pondering that question for about thirty seconds, the senior vice-president said, "You *said* your computer could solve any problem. I suppose we wanted to be convinced that the computer could help us. We've known all this ever since this plant was built, but we haven't been able to convince our two most senior officers that we were right. Yes, I suppose we thought that if your computer told them, they might believe it—even though they wouldn't believe *us*. But now that we think upon it more clearly, that doesn't seem valid."

Tom was almost crushed, but couldn't quite let go. "Why not? I can run these figures through my linear programming package, and the computer will give you a terrific report—even printed with lots of mathematical symbols that can't fail to convince your executives. Just give me a chance."

TOM TIRELESS TINKERS WITH TOYS

The executive continued, hardly noticing the interruption. "No, they simply aren't going to move, regardless of the cost to the company. They can afford it. We three, on the other hand, would like to see our business run more efficiently—we haven't yet made *our* fortunes."

And thus Tom Tireless learned lesson number one in problem definition for those who would presume to solve problems for others:

IN SPITE OF APPEARANCES, PEOPLE SELDOM KNOW WHAT THEY WANT UNTIL YOU GIVE THEM WHAT THEY ASK FOR.

19

PATIENCE PLAYS POLITICS

Sometimes people know perfectly well what they want, but the problems of the solution-problemer don't end there. Consider this story of another computer person, Patience Prudent.

The governor of one of the United States of America had issued orders for all departments of the state government to begin making use of the excellent computers he had, in his infinite wisdom, just purchased for the state. Not that *computers* object to being idle 18 hours a day—they were utterly indifferent, as only a computer can be. But the governor's advisors opined that so much "idle" time might be poor politics in an election year. People value computers not for what they do, but for the amount of time they take doing it. Any problem that takes but a few minutes can't be very important. It was necessary to consume as many hours of computer time as the bureaucracy could manage.

The director of the state's computing center designated one of his programmers as liaison with each department. Patience was assigned to the treasurer's office—one of the few that had no previous computer usage whatsoever. An assistant treasurer gave her the first problem—the allocation of road building assessments among the property owners who stood to benefit from each new road.

PATIENCE PLAYS POLITICS

What Patience had originally estimated to be a week's effort had stretched out to three months, primarily because of an unceasing stream of slight changes by the treasurer. By the time she felt she had the final version, Patience was nearly exhausted, and so was her patience. The treasurer, however, was still not satisfied. "What kind of a program is this?" he asked loftily. "Your total payments come to $13,258,993.24; but the total to be allocated is $13,258,993.25!"

Patience tried to keep her cool. "That's just a result of the differences in rounding the individual amounts. Sometimes the total will be off by a penny, but sometimes it will be exact. In any case, it can never be off by more than a penny, so it's nothing to be excited about—one penny in thirteen million dollars."

"You let me be the one to decide what to be excited about, young lady," the treasurer interrupted. He always seemed to get excited anyway—in the presence of young ladies, *competent* young ladies. "*I* am the one who has the responsibility for the taxpayers' money in this state, not you. And *I* have to answer for *every* penny."

Patience might have been intimidated by his overbearing manner and tone, but she was nearing the end of her tether. "Well, if you ask me, you just don't know your job. Reprogramming this entire job for one diddly little penny won't save the taxpayers anything at all."

"Now don't get excited." The treasurer was deathly afraid of an aroused woman. "There are laws, and I must follow them—to the penny. Regardless of what kind of trouble it causes you and your computer."

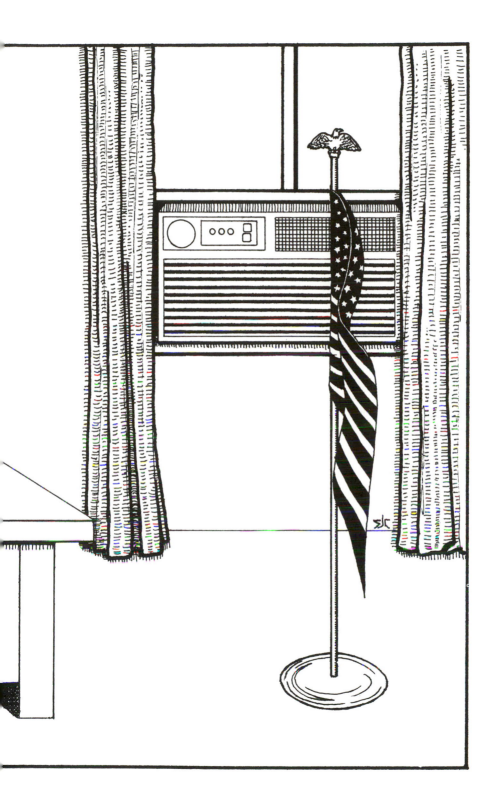

Sensing his fear, Patience had the courage to think clearly about the situation. "But just a minute. How many times each year do you intend to run this program?"

"I can assure you, young lady, that I don't intend to run it at all—unless and until you get it right."

Boiling inside, she strained to keep a calm exterior. "For the sake of argument, let's assume I'll get it right—eventually. Then how many times will you use it?"

"The state makes such assessments approximately ten times per year. In fact, I spend the greater proportion of my time calculating these assessments..."

"I see," Patience interrupted, fumbling around in her purse, and making the assistant treasurer even more nervous. Finding what she sought, she rose to leave. She laid a dollar bill on his desk, saying, "I'd like to make this small donation to the state. You can send me a receipt later." As she moved toward the door, she hesitated, smiled warmly, and said in her sweetest tones, "I guess that finishes the programming. My donation should take care of the legal requirements for the next ten years or so. When it runs out, you can let me know, and I'll make another donation."

Of course, Patience never thought she had solved the assistant treasurer's problem. She was right. He reported to the treasurer that computers could not do the tax assessment with the required accuracy. After wasting three valuable months of his time on the project, he had decided that the best course was to forget about the computer altogether. That, of course, was the solution to his *true* problem.

Neither the problem solver nor the solution problemer is immune to this form of sabotage to her efforts. Patience had learned lesson number two of problem definition:

NOT TOO MANY PEOPLE, IN THE FINAL ANALYSIS, REALLY WANT THEIR PROBLEMS SOLVED.

20

A PRIORITY ASSIGNMENT

One of the finest problem solvers we know got his start cracking codes for an agency whose very *name* was a secret. Over almost a decade of puzzle solving, he acquired considerable skill—a skill that was finally rewarded with a "PRIORITY" assignment.

His mission, with security name JACTITATION, was to "crack" the diplomatic code of "a small European power"—which happened to be an "ally" of his country. JACTITATION was to prove a two-year odyssey, but for over 18 months he seemed to be making no progress at all. Finally, through meticulous tabulations, aided by the world's most powerful computing equipment, he began to be convinced that the diplomats were using a "book code"—a type that is virtually impossible to break.

Another six months of JACTITATION convinced him that the book on which the code was based must be a mystery novel. Two more months narrowed down the probable author. Then, at last, he found the book in the agency's comprehensive library of works of espionage and intrigue—*The Unpleasantness at the Bellona Club,* by Dorothy L. Sayers.

He could hardly contain his eagerness to decode messages. Taking one he thought to be of extreme urgency, he began to translate the meaningless numbers into page, line, and word:

A PRIORITY ASSIGNMENT

PAGE	LINE	WORD	WORD AT THAT LOCATION
112	25	7	TWENTY
133	25	7	THREE
157	27	5	BOTTLES
147	14	6	SCOTCH
19	5	7	FIFTY
32	30	2	NINE
192	17	4	WINE

"Twenty-three bottles Scotch, fifty-nine wine..." It was an expense account! Amused, he tried another message— another expense account! Two days later, he had translated 57 JACTITATION messages—every one an expense account! Two weeks later, our problem solver left the "intelligence" business for a career in teaching.

Before we close our opening, before we end our beginning, we should raise one more question that every would-be problem resolver should ask before seriously embarking on *any* problem:

DO I REALLY WANT A SOLUTION?

Though the question seems shocking, we've already seen a number of instances where the "solution" wasn't at all welcome, once it arrived. It may put the solvers out of a job, as in disarmament—though there we'd hope the other consequences were worth it. Or, as in the JACTITATION caper, the solution may be so trivial in its value that it makes us feel worthless.

ARE YOUR LIGHTS ON?

We get trapped, quite often, because we've worked on a problem so long and so hard that we never really thought we'd solve it—so why worry about whether we want it or not? Conversely, the problem comes upon us too fast for us to consider much of anything about the problem, let alone whether we want the solution. While a poor student window-shops without enough money in his jeans to buy a pack of matches, he dreams about owning a cabin cruiser or, at least, a pack of cigarettes. When he suddenly wins $100,000 in the lottery, his impulse will be to buy each thing he desires, though he may prove susceptible to seasickness or, at least, lung cancer.

Though many problems must be solved in haste, beware of someone pushing you to hurry. Late in the resolution process, haste makes mistakes; in the first few minutes, haste makes disasters. Life is full of variations of the tale of the Fisherman's Wife:

The Fisherman finds a bottle entangled in his net. When the bottle is opened, a Genie escapes and tells the Fisherman that in return for freeing the Genie, the Fisherman and his Wife can have three wishes granted. The couple is, quite understandably, rather excited by the prospect. They sit up late that night discussing their dreams. In their exhilaration, they neglect their supper, so at about three in the morning the wife sighs and mutters, "I'm awfully hungry. I sure wish I had a sausage."

POOF! On the table is a delectable sausage, but the Fisherman is not pleased. "Look what you've done, you foolish woman! You couldn't keep your wits about you, so now we have only two wishes left. I wish that stupid sausage were hanging from the end of your nose."

POOF!

POOF

The reader, experienced in wish situations, can imagine how the third wish was used. At least the Fisherman and his Wife came out better than some of the other three-wishers, like the couple in the ghastly story, "The Monkey's Paw."

An old problem-solving saw goes:

**WE NEVER HAVE ENOUGH TIME TO
DO IT RIGHT, BUT WE ALWAYS HAVE ENOUGH TIME
TO DO IT OVER.**

But because we don't always have the *opportunity* to do it over, we must do better. Put another way,

**WE NEVER HAVE ENOUGH TIME TO CONSIDER
WHETHER WE WANT IT, BUT WE ALWAYS HAVE
ENOUGH TIME TO REGRET IT.**

Yet even when we *do* want the solution itself, we may not notice that there are *inevitable* auxiliary consequences that must accompany *any* solution. One of the ancient quests of the alchemists was the "universal solvent," a liquid whose powers of disintegration could be resisted by no substance on earth. Like the quest for transmutation of lead into gold, this one seems to have been in vain. Too bad, though, because it would have been fascinating to know what they would have kept it in, once they had it!

If we seek a universal solvent, we can hardly deem it a "side effect" that it dissolves any container we try to keep it in—presumably etching a hole through the center of the earth.

A PRIORITY ASSIGNMENT

Yet we tend to regard "side effects" as the result of particular solutions. "They might not arise at all, and if they do, we can always refine the solution to eliminate them." How often does this naive attitude lead us into disaster?

If we set out to eliminate one cause of death after another, why are we surprised at the "side effect" of an increasing population of old people nobody wants? If we set out to eliminate causes of infant mortality, why are we shocked and dismayed when the overall population begins to blossom?

Part of the answer is the human propensity for *habituation: the successive reduction of response to a repetitive stimulus.* Habituation allows us to cancel out the *constancies* in our environment, thus simplifying our lives. When something new appears in our little universe, it is most stimulating. After it remains a short time, offering neither threat nor opportunity, it becomes part of the "environment," or background. Eventually, it is cancelled out entirely:

THE FISH IS ALWAYS THE LAST TO SEE THE WATER.

When we contemplate problems, items to which we are habituated tend to be omitted from consideration. Only when the "solution" causes the removal of the habituated element do we become startled. A most touching representation of this removal phenomenon was shown in Satajit Ray's movie trilogy, *The World of Apu*, when Apu's wife dies.

When he receives the news, Apu casts himself upon the bed, unable to move for days. Ray shows him lying immobile for what seems to the viewer to be hours when, suddenly, the alarm clock *stops* ticking.

ARE YOUR LIGHTS ON?

Apu is startled out of his lethargy and the viewer—who has also been habituated to the ticking—shares the thunderous impact of the sudden *absence*. Only later do we realize that we have been made to share the shock felt by Apu when he realized—after her heart no longer beat—how much his wife had been a part of his life.

Like the filmmaker, the problem resolver is an artist dealing with imaginary worlds. Very early on—really from the very beginning—the problem resolver must strive to see the "water" in which the other participants unconsciously swim—the water which will be transmuted to sand when the "problem" is "solved".

POSTSCRIPT: *By becoming immersed in the problem, the resolver risks yet another oversight. Fascinated with the problem-solving aspects, you may neglect to consider whether you would morally approve of a solution. One person's sin is another's virtue. We wouldn't dare tell any reader that killing people is wrong, any more than we would dare tell a cannibal that eating people is wrong. Perhaps, even at some risk of appearing maudlin, we should quote Polonius:*

"This above all, to thine own self be true."

To be true to yourself, in this business, you must consider moral questions before you get close to a solution, or even a definition, and thereby begin to lose your sensibility. Such consideration will never waste your time, for problem-resolving can never be a morally neutral activity—no matter how much it fascinates its practitioners.

THE FISH IS ALWAYS THE LAST TO SEE THE WATER.

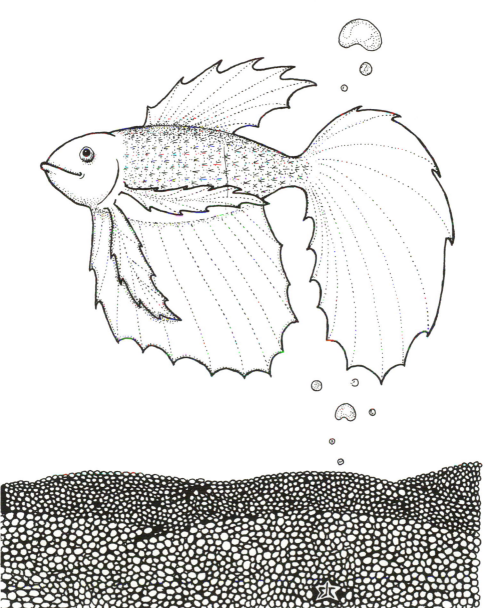